THE WATERS BETWEEN US

THE WATERS BETWEEN US

A Boy, a Father, Outdoor Misadventures,
and the Healing Power of Nature

MICHAEL J. TOUGIAS

LYONS
PRESS

Essex, Connecticut

An imprint of Globe Pequot, the trade division of
The Rowman & Littlefield Publishing Group, Inc.
4501 Forbes Blvd., Ste. 200
Lanham, MD 20706
www.rowman.com

Distributed by NATIONAL BOOK NETWORK

British Library Cataloguing in Publication Information available

Library of Congress Cataloging-in-Publication Data

Names: Tougias, Mike, 1955- author.
Title: The waters between us : a boy, a father, outdoor misadventures, and the healing power of
    nature / Michael Tougias.
Description: Guilford, Connecticut : Lyons Press, 2021.
Identifiers: LCCN 2020045286 (print) | LCCN 2020045287 (ebook) | ISBN 9781493057603
    (cloth) | ISBN 9781493057610 (epub) | ISBN 9781493071845 (paperback)
Subjects: LCSH: Tougias, Mike, 1955- | Outdoor life—Massachusetts. | Nature—Psychological
    aspects. | Fathers and sons—Massachusetts—Biography. | Massachusetts—Biography.
Classification: LCC GV191.42.M4 T68 2021 (print) | LCC GV191.42.M4 (ebook) | DDC
    796.509744—dc23
LC record available at https://lccn.loc.gov/2020045286
LC ebook record available at https://lccn.loc.gov/2020045287

To my dad, Arthur Tougias

Prologue

I ONCE READ THAT ADVENTURE IS THE RESULT OF INEPTITUDE. I HAD lots of adventures. It's the trips that didn't go as planned, the days when nature threw a curve—those are the days I remember best. The days that went well and could be called successful are long since forgotten in the gray haze of marching time. But, oh, those lessons I learned the hard way—those seem like yesterday. Through each misadventure there was a bit of valuable learning that I didn't fully appreciate until adulthood. When I think back on the episodes in this book, I realize the lessons learned help me in my everyday life.

Many of the adventures caused my father to question my sanity and tested his patience. During my boyhood and into my teens, I was a wild kid and a magnet for trouble. Despite our differences I instinctively knew my father loved me, but I felt he didn't like me. There's a difference, and being liked was what I craved at the time.

There were moments when the divide between father and son ebbed and we'd have a real connection, a real conversation. These usually happened when we were fishing with my brother. But the thaw in our relationship was often shattered when I'd get myself in a new tangle of trouble. He wondered why I always had to push the limits, the boundaries, and the rules. I wish I could find the words to tell him, but I had no idea what drove me.

I did, however, have a goal. As far back as I can remember, I wanted a cabin in the mountains, a place to call my own. I didn't know it at the time, but all my explorations in the woods were feeding this dream, making it something of an obsession. During quiet times I sketched pictures of what I thought my cabin and its land should look like. Even at a young age I innately knew that if I wasn't close to nature—at least periodically—something was missing. I'd lie in bed at night thinking of all the wonderful adventures I'd have at this imaginary cabin. And I hoped when my father visited the cabin, we'd finally develop the deeper relationship I craved.

Instead, a family tragedy shook our world, and my father's remarkable response to this event caused me to step back and see the man he was. By observing him throughout this ordeal, I too became a man.

And the cabin? The idea of it was like a smoldering fire that no amount of heartache could extinguish, and when the yearning came roaring back, I found an unlikely ally. Although my father's new burden meant he likely would never see it, he gave me a loan and I bought a cabin in the mountains.

It looked remarkably like the pictures I used to draw.

CHAPTER ONE

THE MEADOWS WERE ONLY FIVE MILES AWAY FROM OUR SUBURBAN Massachusetts home, but to my brother Mark and me, these low-lying acres were in a different world. It was here that our passion for the out-doors blossomed. Filled with marsh, fields, ponds, and streams, the area held infinite possibilities for two young explorers.

And there was mystery too. The Connecticut River, New England's largest, flowed silently, forcefully, by the edge of the Meadows, like a living being that commanded respect by its very presence. We knew little about the river; we had never been on it in a boat, never fished it, and never swum in its dark waters. It was simply too big for us. In fact, the widest point on the river's entire 409-mile length is at the Meadows. To Mark and me it was an ocean—a bit frightening, but a powerful lure nevertheless.

There was one June day in particular that put the Meadows and the river in my heart forever, probably the start of the journey that led me to my quest for a cabin in the woods.

Back in the 1960s, kids could enjoy carefree hours on their own, and on this day Mark and I, ages ten and twelve, enjoyed adventures I'd never let my kids do in today's world. Our plan was to spend a whole day at the Meadows, hiking to see the beckoning river and then fish Longmeadow Brook. We insisted on starting our journey before dawn, because that's when you caught the big ones—or so the fishing mag-azines said. Most parents might have a little trouble waking their kids at 4:30 a.m., but for my father, the baker, that ungodly hour was the normal start to his day.

He roused us while it was still dark, and we stumbled out of bed toward the kitchen, where we ate our Corn Flakes like zombies. I remember a fleeting thought passing through my mind that Dad must have eaten alone like this every day. It never occurred to me to acknowl-edge his years of early-morning labor; now, looking back, I wish I had said a simple thank-you.

Dad drove us through the dark streets, first pointing out where a police car always hid, later putting the high beams on a raccoon crossing the road. We passed the town green and turned downhill toward the Meadows, the headlights now cutting through a thick fog.

When he pulled over to let us out, we hesitated. Although we had made elaborate plans for our trip, we hadn't counted on it being dark when we arrived.

"Well," sighed my father, glancing from our faces then out into the gloom, "you better wait here with me until there's enough light to see."

"But what about the bakery? Doesn't Albert have the mixer going, waiting for you?"

"I can wait with you guys."

"That's OK," I said, still sitting in the front seat, "we'll be fine. The sun will be up soon."

Mark didn't say anything. I was kind of hoping he might have changed his mind and want to go home—then I could curse him for being a chicken and still crawl back into a warm, safe bed.

"At least the fishing should be good," Dad said flatly. He was wearing his usual bakery garb of white pants and white T-shirt over his slender frame.

I forced myself to open the door, and Mark did the same in the back seat. We unloaded our backpacks and rods.

My father, still in the car with the windows rolled down, stared at us standing in the dark. "Why don't I take you back home and you can ride your bikes down later in the morning?"

It was a question, not a command. I looked at Mark, but he made no move to answer. The ball was in my court, and all I could think of was the warm bed back home. But the trip was my idea. "Naw, we'll be OK."

My father turned on the overhead light and glanced at his watch. "It will be light any minute," he said more to himself than us. "Alright, just stay together and don't wander far from the road. I'll pick you up right here at 3:00 p.m. sharp." Then he paused and said, "Michael, do me a favor and don't do anything foolish. Your job is to take care of your brother."

He had emphasized the word "foolish," and I think I knew why. I could still hear my mother screaming on the phone, "Art! Michael split Mark's head open!" Just a few days earlier, Mark and I had gone charging down the hall toward the bathroom, colliding at the door. I flung Mark

3

out of the doorway, and as he fell his head hit the protruding corner of the hallway wall. Blood gushed from the back of his skull onto the beige shag carpet. My mother came running, and the next thing I knew she, crying uncontrollably, had Mark in the car and was on the way to the hospital. All of that because I wanted to be the first to use the bathroom. Foolish.

I felt awful about what I had done, and when they returned— Mark's hair had been shaved at the back of his head, and he sported several stiches—I tried to make things right. I apologized and gave him one dollar.

When my father got home he exploded, shouting that I was older than Mark and that all I did was cause trouble. He also pointed out that giving Mark a dollar wasn't going to make the pain I caused go away.

Now, as Mark and I watched the taillights on my father's Bonneville get fainter, we were left wondering what to do in the pitch dark. Fishing was out of the question, since we couldn't see our fishing rods, let alone the stream. The only way we knew we were in the Meadows was by the smell of the dank air. Earthy, swampy odors are not unpleasant to me, but I remember thinking the smell seemed "prehistoric." My young mind equated this with the giant snapping turtles that were known to live in the ooze that covered so much of the lowlands.

Strange rustling noises came from the woods behind us—probably just night critters—but we decided to follow my father's advice and stay by the dirt road. I thought I would break the tension by engaging Mark in some small talk: "Remember the giant snapper we found in the Eisners' pool?"

Mark didn't answer. I could not see his brown eyes, only the outline of his body. He sat right down on the side of the road. I thought he was going to cry.

Kids react to fear in different ways, but I had never seen a response like Mark's. He opened up our pack, pulled out his lunch, and started eating.

Maybe he wasn't afraid at all; maybe he was bored by being stranded in the dark. I forgot about the snappers and sat down next to him. I too began to eat the sandwich my mother had so carefully packed.

By 5:10 a.m. almost all our food was gone and we were still huddled together in eerie darkness. This was not the way we had planned the big trip.

Have you ever been up at night, waiting for the first gray streaks of dawn? I'm convinced the hours between 3:00 and 6:00 a.m. have a time of their own—a time so slow, you would think there was no time at all. I thought life would be forever frozen at 5:10.

So we sat there, not talking, just watching the sky for a hint of light. I later found out each of us was thinking the same thing. We thought about how different these Meadows were at night, realizing this setting was a bit more formidable than the little patch of woods we played in by our house. Those woods seemed tame compared to this primordial floodplain.

One thought that crossed my mind concerned the tale of a tunnel dug from the center of town all the way to the Meadows. The story claimed the tunnel was built by colonial settlers as a secret escape route in the event of an Indian attack. And it was true that settlers in our town were attacked by Native Americans during King Philip's War, so I always believed the tunnel was built right after that first raid. Now I was worried that we were sitting near the end of the tunnel—I half expected a trap-door to spring open and something ghoulish to pop out.

The morning did not break forth with a burst of light. It was not even a transition into soft light. The sky merely changed from jet black to charcoal gray. If waiting for dawn is slow, this passage from black to gray was maddeningly so.

About twenty minutes later there was enough light to see. We were engulfed in the color green. That's how thick and lush the foliage was. We often think of the summer as vividly colorful. Maybe so at the beach, but on that early morning in the Meadows, there was an absence of all other colors except green, which made it look and feel like a jungle.

We put our packs on and made our way along the trail to the Connecticut River. The jungle gave way to open fields and marsh. The sun was out now, and even at that early hour we knew it was going to be a hot, humid day. Wisps of mist rose off the water and then evaporated in the sun's rays. A lone tree stood in the middle of a broad, flat field, giving the area the look of a savanna. I would not have been surprised to see a giraffe, or maybe a lion stalking a gazelle.

At the end of the field we saw what appeared to be a little hut. Mark started for it, but I tugged his sleeve. "Hobo's hut," I whispered. The railroad tracks from Hartford to Springfield passed nearby, and we had heard of hoboes setting up camp in the Meadows. Mark cocked his head, clearly torn between curiosity and caution. I hoped he wouldn't press the matter.

We stood for a few minutes, just looking at the four-foot-high, box-shaped hut, and I thought about the hobo that might live there. I imagined him cooking hot dogs and beans over an open fire at night then sleeping to the sounds of whip-poor-wills and the hoot of owls. The romance of it all made me wish we had a hut of our own, and I made a mental note to talk to my father about building one. If a hobo could do it, why couldn't we? I pictured a little log cabin with a crackling fire in a stone fireplace. Maybe we would build it right here in the Meadows, a kind of base camp from which to set off on explorations. Or maybe it could be in the mountains or on a lake. When you're twelve, all things seem possible.

We gave the hut a wide berth and continued our westward trek toward the river. The vegetation changed again as we got closer to the water. Towering cottonwood trees blocked out the sky, and there was little undergrowth beneath them, giving this bottomland a park-like appearance. We could see the slow current of the mighty Connecticut ahead, a strange mix of brown and dark blue-black water rippling and shining under the sun.

At the river's edge we paused and just stood staring for several seconds. The humidity gave the air above the water a milky haze, and the opposite shore seemed miles away. Thick tree trunks leaned out over the river, collecting full sunshine instead of climbing straight up and competing with their neighbors. Various items of flotsam had washed up on the bank, and a nearby tree root looked like a fat snake.

We had a healthy respect for the river. True, it delivered its bounty to us from time to time, such as the carp that were trapped inland during receding floodwaters or the three-foot lamprey eels that swam up the feeder streams in the spring. We always discovered those carp and eels in the nearby ponds or streams, while the river itself was a whole different matter. Anything could lurk in there.

Longmeadow is at the southern end of western Massachusetts, so the south-flowing river has already passed through all of Massachusetts, as well as along the borders of Vermont and New Hampshire. The broad expanse of the Connecticut overwhelmed us, making us feel small and insignificant as we cast our lines into its dark, murky water.

Big rivers meant big fish—or so we thought. We cast spinners, jitter-bugs, and spoons. Our small tackle box was filled with metal hardware, most ordered from a TV show featuring "Gadabout Gaddis." But we lost confidence quickly. With so much water in front of us, we figured the fish could be anywhere, and they certainly were not within our casting range.

Mark wandered the shore, and when he returned I was sitting on a log smoking—or trying to smoke—a cigarette. Mark was astonished, having stopped in his tracks when he saw me blow smoke out through my nose.

"What are you doing?" he asked.

"Having a smoke," I answered as cool as possible.

"Where did you get the cigarette?"

"Jerry Roberts. And make sure you don't tell a soul."

"I won't, but you sure look weird. How many times have you smoked one of those?"

"I've probably had close to a pack in the last few weeks. Didn't you know Mommy caught me at the corner of Williams Street and Laurel Street?"

Mark shook his head.

I explained how I had the worst luck imaginable. There I was hanging out at a street intersection with Jerry Roberts, each of us puffing away like we owned the world. He was blowing smoke rings, and I was trying. We thought we looked as tough as the Marlboro Man, especially the way we let the cigarettes dangle from our mouths while we tried to talk. Then we noticed a car slowing down directly in front of us, and in an instant I knew I was in big trouble. Of all the people in the world to drive by that street corner at that particular moment, it had to be my mother. The weird thing was she never stopped the car, just made sure she identified me 100 percent, then kept driving. But I knew I wasn't off the hook. She told my father when he got home from work, and he shouted at me: "You think you're being cool? You're acting like a punk! Go to your room and think about it." I had to stay in my room for the rest of the day, and was not allowed to leave the house for a week. But by driving my mother absolutely nuts, I was able to get her to commute my sentence to three days, which she did just to get me away from her.

Mark was stunned that he didn't even know about this whole incident, especially since we shared a bedroom with our younger brother, Bob: all three beds lined up in a row, completely filling the room. Mark asked a million questions, and for the first time I think I answered them all rather than telling him to get lost. We actually talked like two close friends. I even confided to him that my friends and I had twice pilfered a case of beer from homeowners who left their garages open. I explained what it felt like to be drunk—how you became dizzy, brave, and funny all at the same time. For added impact I described how a certain girl let my friend Jerry and me touch her breasts. And I told him how half the school knew what we were doing and how good it felt to do stuff other kids wouldn't. I was establishing myself as a risk-taker, and basked in the attention.

<hr>

When our discussion of beer, cigarettes, punishments, and how strange we thought our parents were was over, we decided to head to a nearby pond. It was only ten o'clock, but we were ready for lunch. Of course our lunch had been eaten five hours earlier, so we ate the last of our provisions—two apples. When the apples were gone, we discussed whether we could make it till 3:00 p.m. without any more food. It seemed impossible, and we set about the job of catching fish with renewed vigor.

Mark and I were not all that close back then. With the usual sibling rivalries, and my insistence on playing the role of the older brother, it was hard to connect. But on that day we worked as a team—Lewis and Clark had nothing on us. It didn't matter that we could walk three miles to the east and find a phone to call our mother. We were on our own, confident in our abilities, and as a team we focused our attention on catching lunch.

Two hours later we sat side by side, roasting a nine-inch bullhead over a roaring fire. With a fish that size, we could have used a cigarette lighter to cook it, but making a fire was one of the reasons we had come. It made no sense to create such an inferno—we had no pig to roast, and the day was hot and humid—but given half an excuse, boys (and men) will make a fire.

The lone bullhead, a member of the catfish family, was all we caught. We lost most of our appetite trying to kill the damn thing—it seemed like it was as strong out of the water as in it.

Now I know catfish are considered good eating in the South, and I know Southerners fry it rather than roast it on a stick, but nothing will ever convince me to eat one again. And it was difficult to take a bite, because we kept expecting it to start flopping around again.

As the older brother, I thought it was crucial to catch something big on this trip so we could call it a success. I'm sure Mark already considered this one of our better adventures, and he would have been content to explore, see new places, and enjoy the freedom of being a boy in the Meadows. But I was showing signs of adulthood. Bad signs. I was equating success of the trip with something I could show (like a fish) rather than the experience itself. I was becoming goal oriented, perhaps the biggest mistake we Americans teach our kids. The journey itself should have been my fulfillment rather than a big fish. A big fish at twelve years old, a big car at twenty-five, and a big house at thirty. The older we get, the more we lose touch with the important things, which often are the simple pleasures right in front of us.

<hr />

We made our way to a brook where I knew some large suckers lived. The summer heat was now intense, and when we arrived Mark took off his sneakers and put his feet in the stream, letting the cool water refresh him.

I then ruined his fun by saying, "That's the exact spot where a kid killed a twenty-pound snapper."

It was true. I had seen an older boy shoot the snapping turtle with a bow and arrow. The arrow went right through the turtle's neck. It was an awful sight—the arrow prevented the snapper from pulling its head back into its shell, and I had nightmares about the turtle's struggles.

Immediately, Mark had his feet out of the water, his sneakers back on, and was casting nervous glances along the stream bank. We started fishing, using worms with weights attached to the line to keep the bait down where the suckers sucked. I'm not sure what they suck, but suck they do; just look at their mouths sometime.

Then we waited. And waited. And waited some more. We were about to pack up our gear and move on when we heard a voice from behind us.

"What are you guys doing here?" It was Opie. Opie lived only a half mile from the Meadows and spent countless hours poking about. We had been friends for years, always competing, always looking for a thrill.

He was with another friend, Cogs, each riding a Playboy bike and carrying a fishing rod.

"Don't even bother," I said to Opie as I reeled my line in for the last time.

"Did you get anything?" he asked, taking my position on the stream bank.

While I shook my head no, Opie pitched a worm into the head of the pool where a few rocks created riffles, then he continued his interrogation, "How long you been here?"

"Since early this morning, we got one catfish at a different spot."

"You mean to tell me you've been here all day and only caught one catfish?"

It occurred to me that Opie had done nothing but ask annoying questions, and I was getting angrier by the second.

"Well, we also did a lot of hiking, we walked down to . . ."

My excuse was cut short mid-sentence because Opie's rod suddenly arched over. He had a fish on, a good-size fish.

"Wow!" all four of us gasped at once as the fish jumped completely out of the water. This was no sucker. We gathered around Opie and hollered our advice.

"Bring it in, quick!"

"Loosen your drag!"

"Let 'em run!"

"Bring it in, quick!"

"Set your drag!"

"Bring it in, quick, you idiot!"

Cogs entered the water with a net large enough to haul up a tuna. The stream was only six feet wide, and it was easy wading. Opie reeled furiously, and Cogs scooped the fish up: a sixteen-inch rainbow trout!

Mark and I stood with mouths open. None of us had ever caught a trout here, and this was a monster. I remember staring at the bright ribbon of pink along the trout's fat flanks, thinking how strange it was such a beautiful creature came out of that dark little stream.

Opie didn't wait for us to compliment him. He hopped on his bike and rode off with the fish to show his parents and the rest of his neighborhood.

Mark and I went in the other direction to meet our father. We had been in the Meadows for almost eleven hours. Opie had been there five minutes. Already we were planning our next trip, deciding what new lures to buy, and reminding ourselves that we must bring a huge net. And I'd ask Dad about building a small hut near where Opie caught his fish or any place he wanted, so long as it was in the woods and near water. The idea made so much sense to me that I was already thinking about old pieces of furniture to put in it.

Years later I reminded Opie of the big fish he caught. We had a long talk, and the moments and the events of the day came flooding back. I told him how special that day was for me—a day I put aside all sibling rivalries with my brother, a day we were friends, and how my father seemed surprised neither of us got hurt.

I also told him how jealous I was of his trout.

Then Opie said something that made that magical day seem even better.

"We cooked that big rainbow up that night, and all I remember was that it tasted like mud."

CHAPTER TWO

WE TOLD MY DAD ALL ABOUT OUR DAY AT THE MEADOWS, LEAVING OUT the part about the hobo shack. The last thing we wanted to do was have my parents put a crimp on our exploration of the Meadows, especially now that we knew trout lived in Longmeadow Brook. I did, however, ask my father to help build us a hut or little cabin by the brook, but I'd neglected two minor problems: We didn't own the land, and my dad couldn't build a birdhouse, much less a cabin.

My father wasn't exactly handy, nor was he an outdoorsman, having grown up in the city of Springfield, Massachusetts. He didn't know much about fishing, had never hunted, and couldn't tell an oak tree from a maple. Yet despite his lack of knowledge, he truly enjoyed the outdoors.

Although Mark and I didn't know it at the time, we were probably fortunate he was not an outdoorsman. There were no speeches that started out: "When I was a boy, we caught dozens of three-pounders." Consequently, Mark and I never knew what we were missing compared to the "good old days." And we never had to listen to any "expertizing." The few times I did catch a big fish and take it home, Dad's typical comment was "Wow, what is it?"

My father was the son of Greek immigrants, and he made no bones about the fact that he barely got through high school. During his teenage years he often worked in his father's bread bakery when he wasn't in school, and upon graduation he served in the army at the end of World War II and was stationed in postwar Japan. After his time in the military, he returned to the bakery and would work there for the next forty years with his brothers.

When Dad was twenty-two he married my mother, who was only eighteen at the time. She was a short, pretty woman of Italian-Irish descent who was quiet and reserved—the exact opposite of my father. Together they had four children. My sister, Lynn, was the oldest, followed by me, Mark, and my youngest brother, Bob. Because Bob was ten years younger than I, we barely interacted until he was old enough to accompany Mark and me into the woods. But Lynn took him under her wing and was like a second mother to him.

Our family had a middle-class lifestyle, but it came at a tremendous cost. We almost never saw my father because he worked ten hours a day—backbreaking manual labor—five or six days a week. He had very little involvement in our lives, at least compared to the way most parents interact with their kids today. I don't recall my father ever coming to one of my soccer games or wrestling matches, and he never inquired about how we were doing at school and if we studied. In some respects that was a good thing: We learned to be independent and push ourselves when it came to school, sports, and earning money through odd jobs.

Of his four children, I caused him the most grief—by far. In today's world I would have been diagnosed with attention deficit disorder (ADD), but back then I was just a kid who was fidgety, antsy, or "that wild Tougias boy who can't sit still." I was always scheming, planning, and daring my friends to try new things, most of which were semi-dangerous. My mother couldn't really handle me, so with tears in her eyes she'd often say, "I'm telling your father when he gets home." And of course my father would come home exhausted and blow up at me when he heard about the latest incident. Some of those infractions were relatively minor, such as accidently breaking a window playing ball, telling my mother she wasn't the boss of me and I'd do what I pleased, or a neighbor complaining that one of the arrows I shot into the sky was now stuck in their roof. Other issues were more serious, such as notes from the school assistant principal saying I practically lived outside his office because teachers would send me there for making jokes in class. And then there were the neighborhood fights. I was small for my age, but I learned early on that I had quick fists and size didn't always matter. And I actually liked to fight, at least until a kid from the city of Springfield beat the crap out of me at summer camp.

So ours was no idyllic family, and my father never really tried to understand me, or talk to me about why I always seemed to be in trouble. And who could blame him; he had three other kids who acted responsibly, and he was probably sick of working his ass off all day only to get home and learn about my latest escapade or fight. Heck, my very first memory of being alone with my father, around age five, ended with me ignoring his instructions and almost killing myself. We had just moved to Longmeadow, and he still hadn't sold our earlier home in Springfield, so he rented it out. The place was falling apart, and on Saturdays, my father's only day off from work, he took me with him to the Springfield house to give my mother a break from me.

The backyard of that house in the city was surrounded by a chain-link fence, and Dad gave me a bunch of toys and told me to stay in the backyard while he climbed a ladder and scraped peeling paint off the second story. As soon as he was up on the ladder and engrossed in the job at hand, I promptly set about trying to escape the backyard. There was a grand old maple tree across the road with flowers around its base, and I decided I'd climb the tree then pick a bunch of flowers to give to my mother, since she always seemed mad at me. A steady stream of cars whizzed down that road like there was no tomorrow, so maybe what happened next actually saved my life. I scaled the fence and was about to go down the other side when my foot slipped. The fence top had exposed steel barbs crossing like an X, and I became impaled, with one barb slicing into my thigh and another into . . . let's call it a private part.

I let out a scream and saw bright red blood pouring down both legs. I'll never forget looking back at my father way up on the ladder, thinking he was going to fall off. But he scrambled down, extracted me from the fence, placed me in the front seat of the car, and then sped to the emergency room, where they stitched me up. (Yes, I was lucky; I could have been neutered before I even reached puberty.) That was one of many trips to the emergency room for me (and a couple for Mark that I caused). I remember driving home and my father asking me why I was climbing the fence when he told me to stay in the yard. When I told him about the special tree and flowers, he shook his head, saying something like "What the hell am I going to tell your mother? I was supposed to be watching you." And because I was fascinated by Tarzan at that age, I probably answered that I wanted to be in the tree "just like Tarzan." Maybe that's when my father decided to give up trying to understand me.

As a twelve-year-old, I was always curious and frequently annoying, which didn't endear me to my five other family members. My older sister, Lynn, probably took the lion's share of aggravation. It was tough enough being the lone female out of four siblings, but what really got under her skin was when I'd spy on her or eavesdrop on her conversations. Looking back, I can't even remember why I did this, but likely it was just to make myself more of a pest—and also because she was older and her life seemed more interesting.

I'd listen in on Lynn's after-school phone chats by carefully picking up another phone, eavesdrop until she was finished, then I'd hang up with no one the wiser. At the dinner table I'd announce to the family what secrets I'd heard, and Lynn would scream, "Dad, he's snooping on me again; you've got to do something!"

My father would glare at me and shout, "How many times have I told you to leave your sister alone?"

It was a rhetorical question, but I'd answer anyway, "Six?"

"No, it's constant! So this is it; if you listen to her calls again, you're in big trouble."

My father seemed serious, so I tried a different tact. "I didn't mean to. I just picked up the phone to call Cogs, and she was already on it. I hung up after a minute and . . ."

My sister pointed at me. "He did not. He heard the whole call. He's ruining my life. Why does he have to be so annoying!"

I came back with, "Why does she get her own phone in her room? It's not fair."

My father silenced the debate. "Enough! For the last time, leave your sister alone!"

And so I did—until I found a better way to spy on her. This method was absolutely brilliant, if I do say so myself. Our den had a built-in bookcase and cabinet covering almost an entire wall. Bookcases enclosed the top half, a recessed compartment for a TV was in the middle, and on the bottom were two large cabinets where we stored our toys and sports equipment. Mark and I discovered that inside the two cabinets there was no top, but instead two hollow openings that, like the flue of a chimney, went straight up to the ceiling. It was possible for small skinny kids like Mark and me to get inside the cabinet and then, with a bit of effort and gyration, stand up. Mark got in one cabinet and I in the other, and when we stood we could actually see each other's head across an opening that was above the recessed box that held the TV. Even better, we could pull ourselves up and sit together on top of the enclosed TV box, completely hidden inside the wall. Oh, the possibilities of this secret place were endless, and my thoughts turned to Lynn.

"Mark, we can hide up here and listen to Lynn and Mandy (our neighbor) next time we know they are going to be in the den watching TV."

"And we could bring food with us!" said Mark.

"And a tape recorder!"

"Why?"

"To tape Lynn, and blackmail her!"

"I dunno about that . . . ," said Mark.

"Wait!" I hissed. "I've got a better idea. We can make a little hole in the wall right where we are sitting above the TV. Then we could see her or anyone who sits on the couch!"

Mark saw the possibilities. "It could be like watching a movie! We'd have snacks, drinks, and see and hear everything they do!"

A couple months went by before Mark and I had enough lead time to know exactly when Lynn and Mandy were going to be watching a TV show together. My mother was the one who inadvertently tipped us off. "There's a show on TV Lynn and Mandy want to watch after dinner, so leave them alone. You can watch the TV in my room if you want to."

Aha! It was a summer evening, and just before Mandy came over, Mark and I went out the back door to play—only to reenter the house quietly through the front door, slip into the den, crawl up the wall, and take our sitting positions behind the bookshelves about four feet off the ground and just above the TV. The tape recorder had been forgotten, but no matter.

We heard Mandy come in through the back door, and I craned my neck to the peephole. She and Lynn entered the den, turned on the

TV, and took their seats on the couch. They were probably watching one of the shows like *Bewitched* or the *Flying Nun*, both of which Mark and I considered "girl shows," and nowhere near as good as *The Andy Griffith Show*, which had such lovable characters as Barney, Goober, and Ernest T. Bass. Heck, I would have watched *Andy Griffith* for the opening credits just to see Opie carrying out a string of fish from the secluded lake in Mayberry. (My friend Opie was a dead ringer for the one on the TV show.)

Mandy and Lynn, sitting on the couch, did not reveal any state secrets and said nothing of consequence, but Mark and I found the experience fascinating. We whispered back and forth.

"What are they doing now?" asked Mark

"Nothing, but they've got popcorn."

"Let me see, let me see," said Mark. We should have made two holes, but we shared the one we had, and Mark took his turn.

"What's happening?" I hissed in his ear.

"It's amazing," said Mark; "they are looking directly at us and have no idea we're here."

We watched for another five minutes until I accidentally banged an elbow on the wall.

Both Lynn and Mandy leaned forward, perching on the edge of the couch, their eyes searching every part of the room.

"What was that?" asked Mandy.

"I have no idea," said Lynn, "but that was really creepy."

I shined the flashlight directly on Mark's face. He had his hand over his mouth to keep from laughing out loud, and his body was shaking from suppressed giggles.

With Mark ready to burst at any minute, I decided to go for broke. I took a deep breath, placed my tongue against my bottom lip, and let out a long, loud, deep, and very wet fart sound.

The girls screamed, sprang to their feet, and dashed from the room. I looked out the peephole just in time to see my mother walk into the room, followed by Lynn and Mandy.

"Where did the noise come from?" my mother asked.

"From the wall," stammered Mandy; "it's haunted. We heard a bang first."

"Then," added Lynn, "we heard another noise. It was awful. It sounded like a poop, like something farted."

That last line sent me over the edge, and I broke out laughing.

Lynn shouted, "Mom! It's Michael and Mark, they're in the wall! They were spying on us!"

When my father got home, there was hell to pay. I can still see him in his standard white V-neck T-shirt, with smatterings of white flour in his black wavy hair. "How many times have I told you, leave your sister alone!"

"But we were in our fort in the wall, and Lynn and Mandy came in the family room."

"Well, I don't care! Go outside to your real fort, but stay out of that wall."

For a moment I considered saying that if we had a cabin in the mountains, we wouldn't have to hide in the wall. Then I thought better of it. I do wish my father had just talked with me, maybe even asked me why I felt a need to always be causing trouble, always looking for attention at school. Maybe he could have started a conversation by saying something like, "Look, I know you're just trying to have fun, but why not pick your spots?" But that was not his nature, nor was it likely the approach many fathers used back in those days. What I didn't know about my father was that he'd do anything for his kids, and later he would give of himself in a way that few people do. He was about *doing*, but not necessarily discussing feelings or giving pep talks.

My father was a shouter when he was angry, and that shouting often scared me, but it also made me resentful that I couldn't tell my side of the story. Later, I came to the conclusion that he also raised his voice because he was hard of hearing, perhaps due to the clattering equipment at the bakery, and when something important had to be said, he made sure his voice was good and loud. I also came to understand that he was sleep deprived after working ten straight hours on his feet, and coming home to hear a litany of my boorish behavior didn't exactly pick his spirits up. But this insight took years for me to comprehend, and back in the late 1960s we just followed the well-worn trail of father-and-son misunderstandings with no real dialogue. And I simply wasn't bright enough, or maybe too selfish, to see anything beyond my own perspective.

My real angst, however, came from the instinctive feeling that my father didn't like me. And at age twelve that can be devastating when you don't know how to bridge the divide.

The next day Mark and I went to our friend Greg's, who lived two homes away on a road behind the street we lived on. Our backyards almost touched each other's. We had a well-worn path leading from our yard, through a short patch of hemlocks, and on into Greg's yard. We knocked on his door, and his mother answered.

"Can Greg play?" I asked. What a wonderful word, "play." It means everything and nothing at the same time. It's a totally open-ended word, where possibilities are endless. Almost every day in the summer, either Mark or I must have asked if Greg could play, and out he'd come and off we'd go. Looking back, he had a pretty good deal going, because we always went to his house and roused him out of his TV watching. We were doing him a favor by getting him outdoors, but his mother never saw it like that. Greg once told me his mother said, "Those Tougias boys are just a little too wild." I could understand why she thought that way because invariably Greg returned from our outings either injured or with ripped clothing.

Each time Greg came to the door when we knocked, his mother was behind him and would say something like, "Now, Greg, I don't want you going off into the woods and getting hurt. So stay in the neighborhood."

Greg would say, "OK," and then we'd head straight for the woods. Greg was one year younger than I and one year older than Mark, which made him the perfect partner for both of us. He was an easygoing kid, a little on the chubby side, with long brown hair hanging over thick eyeglasses in black frames. His clothing always looked like it was ironed and newly bought. In many ways Greg was more worldly than Mark and I, maybe because he had an older brother. Greg's room was filled with the latest albums, like the Mamas and Papas, Simon and Garfunkel, and all the latest British bands, including the Kinks. I learned more about music from Greg than anyone else, and we must have listened to "Daydream" by the Lovin' Spoonful and "Cherish" by The Association a thousand times. Greg was the one who pointed out that the Kingsmen song "Louie Louie" had a line in it about getting laid; sure enough, after several careful listenings, we distinctly heard it. He also pointed out that when the Rolling Stones went on the *Ed Sullivan Show*, they did not sing the words "Let's spend the night together" but instead had to change it to "Let's spend some time together."

Greg's walls were covered with posters, and he even knew some of the details about the Vietnam War, whereas Mark and I couldn't quite get our heads around it. We saw the body counts of the enemy killed flashed on the nightly news with Walter Cronkite and assumed we were winning, whereas Greg would say things like the whole war is stupid, and he was worried his brother would be sent over there.

───

When Greg came out of his house, we told him about hiding in the wall and how my father shouted at us and told us to go to our real fort, which was basically a few sticks in the hemlocks between our houses. I told Greg I was sick of our fort because a good fort would be one that no one knew about, least of all my father.

"We need a new fort," I said, "somewhere no one knows about."

"Yeah," said Greg; "even my brother knows where we go. But I think I know a place where nobody will find us. Get your bikes and meet me back here; I'll show you."

In the 1960s the bike of choice for boys was the Columbia-made "Playboy" bike. These bikes had high-rise handlebars called monkey bars with curved hand grips and "banana" seats that were about a foot and a half long and five inches wide. My Playboy was green with sparkles, and it's the only bike I ever loved. When I rode that bike I was a mean, bad dude, the coolest kid around.

The only thing that might have made me look cooler was if I could have grown a Fu Manchu mustache or muttonchops, but I did the next best thing and wore tinted granny glasses. And to be extra tough, we often put baseball cards in the spokes so the bikes sounded like motor-cycles. That Columbia Playboy was like having a horse. It had its own personality and took me to adventure. It also took me to school, every day, even during winter, and I saw more of the crossing guard at Williams Street than I did my own sister.

The banana seat was long enough that Mark could fit on the back, and we zipped down Ridge Road, made a left on Primrose Drive, and arrived at Greg's house, where he was waiting on his own bike.

"Follow me!" Greg shouted, happy to be in the lead instead of me. We followed Primrose Drive less than a quarter mile to its intersection with Magnolia Circle, and Greg pulled into a grove of woods that had not yet been stripped for houses. We hopped off our bikes while they were still moving and let them crash into the brush. Greg ran up a dirt embankment and stood at the top.

"Right here, this is it," he said.

"What's so special about this?" I asked, shaking my head in disbelief that this little hill could be made into a fort.

"For one," said Greg, "anyone approaching, especially kids we don't want here, will have to climb this hill. And we could fight them off while staying protected in this trench behind the hill." He pointed to a dip on the back side of the knoll that was about five feet wide before the land rose once again.

"Yes!" shouted Mark; "it's perfect. Nobody will see us in up here, but we'd be able to watch anyone approaching from either side, especially if we climbed this tree."

The tree was a small maple, but it had plenty of low-lying branches and would be easy to climb. I hated to admit it, but Greg had found a good spot. The fact that there was a "Keep Out" sign meant little to us. I'd been breaking what I considered silly rules regularly: "No Jumping," "No Swimming," "No Trespassing" . . . "No Fun." I was learning to access dan-ger; sometimes I made good choices and sometimes bad, but at least I felt free. (I haven't changed much: If I see a "No Trespassing" sign on a beach, I usually keep walking. I don't tread on people's lawns, but I'll be darned—and maybe arrested—before I'll concede that the ocean is only for a few.)

Now most people when they hear the word "fort" conjure up an image of a wall of logs, a roof, and maybe even a palisade, but we used the term rather liberally. We arranged four small logs in a square about five feet wide, and that was our fort. We felt we could defend our garrison against bears, wolves, Indians, and neighborhood kids who didn't know our password. Our password, after much discussion, was ingenious: a four-letter word that began with "F." The password was . . . "fort." Greg voted for another four-letter "F" word, "fart," but Mark and I overruled him, claiming that any kid would guess that within minutes.

Once the fort was built, we elected a leader, sort of. I ran for president unopposed. When the two ballots were counted, one was left blank and the other said "Greg." The printing looked very much like Mark's. I was not pleased, not a single vote for me.

"But Greg doesn't want to be president," I argued.

Before Mark could respond, Greg broke the tension and said he would be fine being vice president of our new club. I quickly seconded that. Then I appointed Mark as "scout."

"What the heck is scout?" Mark asked.

"The scout keeps watch over the fort."

"And is that all?"

"Yeah, but you've got to get up in the tree to see in all directions."

"But I don't want to sit up in a tree all day."

Greg piped in, "How about he only has to be in the tree some of the time?"

Mark was not happy. "I still don't want to be the scout."

"Well, what else is there?" I asked.

"Treasurer," said Mark, "I want to be the treasurer."

"Treasurer! But we have no money, so what would you be treasurer of?"

Greg proposed a compromise. "How about he becomes scout and treasurer, and we each put in a dime as dues?"

We all agreed this made sense. Greg was going to make a fine vice president.

Just then we heard laughter from the woods. We quickly poked our heads above the trench. Standing not less than ten feet away were Lynn and Mandy. "Nice fort!" Lynn shouted, and off they ran.

Mark, Greg, and I looked at one another, shaking our heads. Being successfully spied on was not the way to kick off our new fort. As president I felt I had to do something.

"That," I declared, pointing at the fleeing girls, "is exactly the reason we need Mark to be the scout. We can't be spied on again."

"So," said Mark, "I'm supposed to sit up in the tree and warn you if I see anyone coming?"

"Yes, it will be exciting."

"No, it will be stupid."

Greg moved us along. "We've got to raise money for our club. Let's think up ways we can do it."

We spent a while kicking ideas around, but they all involved doing odd jobs that were way too much work than we were willing to do. Then a thought hit me.

"I know! We can become trappers. We will trap animals and sell their skins."

Without much discussion, Mark and Greg agreed, because the idea sounded more exciting than mowing the Goldbergs' lawn or weeding the Alperts' bushes.

We had no idea how to trap animals, but Greg went home to get a shovel and I went home to find something to use as a trap. I searched both the garage and the basement, and the only thing that caught my eye was a couple of mousetraps. They would have to do.

When I arrived back at the fort, Greg and Mark had already dug a hole two feet deep by three feet wide. They were in the process of covering it over with sticks and branches.

"What's in your hand?" Greg asked, looking up at me.

"Traps."

"They look kind of small."

"I know, but it's all I could find."

Mark was covered in dirt, but I could still tell by his expression that he doubted my sanity.

"What about bait? How are you going to get something to go to your trap?"

I hadn't thought of that, so I tried turning the tables. "Well, how are you going to get something to go in the pit you dug?"

"We dug it on the path, figuring animals use the path at night, just like us."

"OK, but I'm going to need bait for these small traps. Have you guys got anything?"

Mark and Greg shook their heads.

I noticed Greg was chewing gum. "Let's use Greg's gum and see what happens."

And so began our careers as trappers.

The next morning we got Greg out of his house bright and early, eager to see if we had caught anything at the fort. Our first stop, at the pit covered with branches, was a disappointment; nothing had disturbed the camouflage covering, nor was a creature down in the pit. Then we walked over to the spot in the woods where I set the first mousetrap, hoping we caught a rabbit, weasel, or something else larger than the trap.

I looked down at the ground where the trap should have been. "It's gone," I whispered. "It should be right here." Hunched over, Mark and Greg started examining the ground, walking in widening circles.

"Here it is!" Greg shouted. Greg picked up what he thought was an empty trap. Then he screamed and dropped it while jumping backward. At first I thought the trap had sprung on his hand.

Greg was starting to hyperventilate. "There, there's something in it . . . a piece of something."

Mark, Greg, and I slowly converged on the trap for a better look. There was indeed something in it: a leg, a very small leg. Bigger than a mouse but smaller than a squirrel. Maybe a shrew or a chipmunk. We knelt down for a better view.

"Oh, my God," said Mark. "It chewed its own leg off."

We immediately stopped trapping—and suspended all dues to the treasury.

~ ~

A few days later we were back at the fort, and I realized how relaxed I was at this spot; no peer pressure like at school, and no girls. I didn't like living in suburbia—I wanted to be like the kid from *My Side of the Mountain* who lived in a hollow tree deep in the forest. But our fort was the next best thing and close at hand. The good feelings at the fort fueled my thoughts of having a cabin and becoming a mountain man, but the woods surrounding the fort also caused a few harrowing moments, and we were literally about to step into one.

Mark, Greg, and I had a few things hidden under a log twenty feet from the fort: a hatchet, a slingshot, and a moldy *Playboy* magazine wrapped in plastic. You can guess which one we liked best. On this particular day Greg led the way to get the magazine and suddenly let out a blood-curdling scream while jumping straight up into the air. Then there was a faint buzzing sound, followed by more screaming from Greg as he hit the ground running, flailing his arms wildly.

He shot right past Mark and me, and we couldn't believe our eyes. There must have been a hundred hornets behind him, amassed like wave after wave of fighter planes swooping down on an aircraft carrier (Greg) intent on kamikaze attacks. The most amazing aspect of all, however, was that the hornets went right by Mark and me without so much as a single one stopping to sting us. They were zeroed in on Greg. It was he who first stepped on the entrance to their underground hive.

Greg wailed horrific high-pitched screams as he ran, and it didn't take a genius to know that each yell meant he'd been stung once again. Mark and I raced after him.

Greg broke from the cover of the woods and ran right by his bicycle, not daring to stop. I thought the hornets, upon exiting the woods and entering the sunshine, might disperse, but they were streaming behind him in a long arching tail. And directly around his head swarmed at least twenty-five of the demons, appearing like a veil over his face. It looked exactly like something I'd seen on Saturday-morning cartoons, only there was no mistaking that this was real and terribly painful.

Greg was running so fast I doubt we could have kept up with him, but Mark and I solved that problem by hopping on my bike, with Mark sitting behind me on the banana seat. We rode just behind our screaming friend, but not too close. We shouted inspired but useless words of encouragement as he ran. "They're still on you! Don't stop!"

I doubt he heard us, because the next minute he stopped running, did a pirouette, and then went into a spasmodic dance. I slammed the brakes on my bike so we wouldn't go crashing into him, and we skidded to a halt. I expected the hornets to be gone, but at least half the original number still swirled about Greg, and I wondered why in God's name he had stopped running. Then it hit me. Some of the winged devils must have got up his pant legs and inside his shirt, because he was slapping his body rather than the air around his head. Even from a few feet away, I could see one of his eyes was swollen shut, and his cheeks were so puffy it looked like he was holding in a mouthful of air.

If I had been half a man, I would have thought of something to do to help him. Maybe roll him on the ground like someone on fire. Or I could have gotten Mark off the back of my bike and then ridden by Greg, motioning for him to hop aboard like the cavalry did when one of their comrades was wounded and on the ground. And if I'd had even the smallest amount of brain matter, I would have simply given him my bike. Instead I yelled, "Greg! Run!"

And he did. He was now just a couple of houses away from his own, and the swarm had begun to scatter. Greg was crying, out of breath, and literally staggering. It felt safe to approach him, and while Mark grabbed one of his hands and pulled him along, I raced to his house and yelled for his mother.

She came rushing out, her face a ghastly white, shrieking, "What happened, what happened?" She ran to Greg, wrapping her arms around him while quickly hustling him into the house. She slammed the door behind her.

Mark and I stood outside for a moment, still in shock. But there was nothing we could do now; we slowly walked back to my fallen bicycle and rode home, wondering if Greg was headed to a hospital. We didn't understand anything about allergies to hornet stings; thank God Greg didn't have one, but we knew what we witnessed was serious.

Greg's mother immediately took him to a local doctor, and he recovered quickly. After just twenty-four hours he was up and around, back to his old self. But he wasn't allowed over our house or to the fort for a long time. That didn't surprise me. I knew what his mother had said about us Tougias boys, and I remember her admonition to Greg just an hour before he was attacked: "I don't want you going off in the woods and getting hurt." He had not only gone into the woods but come back a lumpy swollen mess, his face a pincushion for a hundred hornets.

———

Now that I reflect on that one little patch of woods that housed our fort, I realize that several misadventures and close calls occurred there. And maybe that was part of its attraction—any excitement was preferable to boredom. I can't help but feel sorry for the kids today; everything is safe and sanitized, and so much of their leisure time is manufactured by someone else with almost no creativity on their part. They are too often spectators and rarely participants. Greg broke his mother's rule about staying out of the woods and suffered the consequences, but I'll bet looking back on it, he'd say it was worth it.

That same thinking was what attracted me to the idea of a cabin. When people later said to me, "A cabin will be a lot of headaches," I'd think, *That may be, but it will lead to excitement.* I didn't want to just watch other people have fun or read about others' adventures. I wanted my own. I wanted to be engaged with nature . . . just like at the fort. And later I vowed never to put up a "Keep Out" sign—if someone wanted to walk through my land, they would be free to do so.

CHAPTER THREE

By the time the school year started, I was ready for seventh grade, ready for anything and everything, which mostly meant detention. And as 1967 gave way to 1968, I seemed to get in an increasing amount of trouble at school. I'm sure I had attention deficit disorder, but back then I was referred to as unruly and disruptive. I had all this energy that couldn't be burned off in school, so I was easily distracted—which, come to think of it, describes lots of boys. I'm probably the record holder for staying after school at Williams Middle School; for the months of January and February, I had detention *every* day. It got so bad that one teacher, Ms. Ravlo, took pity on me and even offered to drive me home because it was getting dark after detention was over. What a mistake for that poor, kindhearted woman.

I'd never been in a teacher's car before, never been this close to a teacher, and for the first time in my obnoxious twelfth year of life, I had nothing to say. Ms. Ravlo did her best to make small talk as we slowly motored down the long school driveway and cruised out onto the main road. She tried to say that it wasn't too late for me to turn over a new leaf, that I had potential if I could just keep quiet in class.

Then she slammed on the brakes, screamed, and plowed into a dog.

The dog let out a terrible, high-pitched squeal, and in the glow of the headlights I saw it go flying by my passenger side of the car.

Ms. Ravlo stopped the car, started shaking, and was soon crying uncontrollably. Seeing your teacher cry is about as unnerving as anything a student can witness. And being alone in a dark car with a crying teacher is downright terrifying. So I did the only thing I could think of. I cried too.

It wasn't that I was sad for the dumb dog that had run into our path; it was more from being overwhelmed by the entire episode, but particularly from hearing the snorts and wracking sobs of my English teacher.

After two minutes of both of us blubbering and snuffling like three-year-olds, Ms. Ravlo caught her breath. "Do, do, you, you, think the dog is da, dead?" she stuttered.

Hearing her familiar voice rather than the strange weeping and sniveling snapped me out of my own crying bout, and I did the first mature thing I'd ever done.

"I don't know. I saw it kind of twist through the air."

Ms. Ravlo didn't answer. We were parked on the shoulder of the road, with the back of her car sticking out into the street. A couple of cars had already gone by, and one blasted its horn at us, causing Ms. Ravlo to start sobbing again. I had to do something.

"I'll go outside and look for it."

I did not want to do this. It was dusk and difficult to see. There were some woods right next to the side of the road, and I envisioned a couple horrible scenarios. Either the dog was in the woods and would leap at my throat the minute I opened the door, or it was lying right behind the car, still alive but with its guts half out. I wasn't sure which would be worse.

I forced myself to open the door. With shaking legs I stepped outside, absolutely terrified that whatever we hit was going to exact its revenge. Somehow I managed to close the car door, but not all the way—just in case. Then I did something that wasn't quite noble but, considering my fear, was the best I could muster.

I took exactly two steps away from the car, did a cursory glance around, and listened for a moment. Then I told myself, *That's long enough.* I quickly scooted back in the car.

"The dog must be fine," I said. "I looked all around the car, even behind it, and it's not there."

Ms. Ravlo, still shaken, was at least back in control. "Are you sure?"

"Yup," I lied. "You probably just nicked him, and he ran off."

She seemed satisfied and more than a little relieved. Except for my giving directions to my house, the rest of the trip passed in silence. When we pulled in my driveway and I stepped out, I acted like nothing had happened. I just said, "Thanks for the ride, Ms. Ravlo. See you tomorrow."

It was kind of strange to be in Ms. Ravlo's class the next day, and I think for the first time I viewed her as a real person rather than a teacher. Somehow I had thought the two were exclusive. I even cleaned up my act and stayed quiet in class—for all of one week. Then I was back at it, trying—and succeeding—as the class clown.

Finally the school principal sent a letter to my parents. My father, who thought my late arrivals home were because I was playing with friends after school, exploded.

"What the hell! Why are you getting detentions?"

I just shrugged.

My father's face was bright red as he hollered, "Get in your room, and don't come out!"

He followed me to my room and slammed the door shut.

From my room I could hear him talking to my mother, so I opened the door a crack to listen. The gist of what he was saying was "Why can't he just follow the rules like other kids?" My mom answered, "I have no idea, but I can't control him."

When my father was in the army he had been promoted from private to sergeant, and he was damn proud of it. I'm sure he achieved that promotion through self-discipline, and he probably wondered why I couldn't do the same. You might think that having been a sergeant in the army would have made him a strict dad, but his natural tendency was to be easygoing, and he had very few rules and demanded little from us kids. He just wanted me to be like my brothers and sister, to be "good" and listen to my mother and our teachers at school.

So why was I acting up in my classes? Besides my impulsive nature, there was another reason. Girls.

They were the cause, I was the victim. They made me do it. I couldn't help myself. When I made a joke in class, they laughed; it was such a thrill, such a rush, I became like an addict, wanting more of the kick it gave me.

To make matters worse, playing the rebel seemed to work. I had several girlfriends that year, and I loved being with them, loved the attention, loved the feeling of popularity.

Of course all this behavior was giving my parents gray hair. I'll never forget how I arranged to meet my girlfriend Jane at the Lains' house to spend the night together. (Hey, blame it on the Rolling Stones.) And to think Jane and I were just twelve or thirteen years old! (I can't remember what we had planned, since I hadn't even reached puberty. So, Jane, if you're still out there, refresh my memory.) Bobby Lain and his sister

Jamie were twins, and Jane was friends with Jamie, as I was with Bobby. We concocted this scheme that we would sleep over their house on the same night (their parents had no idea Jane and I were a couple). It was a beautifully planned ploy, almost foolproof. But I overlooked the possibility of bad timing, coincidence, and my mother's keen eyesight.

While my mother was driving me to my sleepover at the Lains' house, Jane's mother was driving her there. About a mile from the Lains' place my mother said, "That girl in the blue car ahead of us looks just like Jane."

My heart stopped. Oh, my God, it *was* Jane! It was like watching a car accident starting to develop in slow motion.

"Naw," I said, "looks like her, but they have a different car."

Now the car in front of us turned onto the Lains' street, with us right behind it. Then the blue car turned into the Lains' driveway and my mom did the same.

I panicked, but recovered in time to blurt out, "This is not the Lains' house; it's two more down."

My mother started to speak, "Yes it is, I . . ."

Jane stepped out from the car in front of us. My mother gasped, putting it all together. "Why you! How dare you!"

She had already put the car in reverse and floored the gas pedal, sending us scooting back out into the street.

"I didn't know Jane was going over, I . . ."

My mother cut me off. "Don't say another word! Tell it to your father."

I was so devastated that I wasn't going to spend the night with Jane, I didn't care about my father, my mother, or anyone else. When we got home, my father shouted at me; I was sent to my room, grounded, and I wasn't allowed to use the telephone for a month. My response? I climbed out my bedroom window and ran away to a friend's house. My father tracked me down that same night and dragged me home.

Those were a bad few months. Looking back, I truly feel for my parents; I was spinning out of control—and it wasn't just girls. I was smoking cigarettes, getting in fights, and drinking beer that my friends and I had pilfered from our parents' stock or stolen out of neighbors' garages. I often hung out with a different group of guys than Opie and Cogs, and this new group was a little tougher, more prone to raise hell, break laws, and get in fights. I'm not sure why I went through this stage, but the year 1968 didn't help.

The quagmire in Vietnam dominated the news in 1968, causing incredibly deep divisions in our society, and at times it seemed our country was on the brink of civil war. Kids like me were aware of what was going on with college students who were not only protesting the war but also taking over college administration buildings and daring the authorities to forcibly remove them. I took my cues from the students who were antiestablishment and went out of my way to ignore both teachers and parents. I can remember talking with friends and saying things like "Why even bother worrying about school when we're just going to be drafted and sent to Vietnam as soon as we graduate?"

And it wasn't just students who were against the war. By 1968 even Walter Cronkite, perhaps the most respected TV anchorman, broke his neutrality and explained to a stunned nation that a recent trip to Vietnam had left him deeply disillusioned, and that he now thought the war effort was both immoral and futile.

The nightly images I watched on our grainy black-and-white TV reinforced my belief that the madness in the world was only getting worse. Enemy and US body counts from Vietnam were tallied while video rolled showing horrifying scenes of villages being napalmed, Buddhist monks protesting by self-immolation, and our wounded soldiers being carted off the battlefield. My friend Greg might have been right a year earlier when he said the war was stupid.

Vietnam may have been at the forefront of the turmoil of 1968, but it was by no means the only depressing and disastrous event. That was the year civil rights activist Martin Luther King Jr. was murdered in Memphis, sparking rioting that killed forty-five people and injured more than a thousand. Cities were burning, soldiers were patrolling the streets, and it seemed the very fabric of our society was unraveling before our eyes. Then it got even worse. Senator Robert Kennedy, running as a Democratic candidate for president, was assassinated by a gunman at a hotel just minutes after he gave a victory speech upon his California primary win. Coming on the heels of Martin Luther King's assassination, the two deaths fueled conspiracy theories. And when the Democratic convention was held in Chicago, ten thousand young people descended on the city to protest the war. Police responded with their billy clubs, creating a scene of bloody violence that left me thinking the end of America was near.

Looking back on that year, it's clear the chaos in our society fueled the erratic behavior of many young adults, and I was no exception. Fights with my parents were now becoming a daily occurrence, and my gang of friends continued to court trouble. I wasn't experimenting with drugs or smoking pot yet, but it wasn't for lack of trying. If we had gotten our hands on marijuana or stronger drugs, I'm certain we would have used them, as I did a couple years later. I probably was also buffeted about by new hormones as I entered my teenage years.

Two things helped keep me from going completely off a cliff. Probably the more important one was that my town's school districts were rezoned; I was forced to switch schools and leave some friends behind. At the new school I made new friends, and reconnected with Opie. The change of scenery did me good. Opie had grown his curly red hair into a kind of white-man's Afro and was finding his share of trouble, but he was naturally smart and still gave schoolwork at least some of his attention. His grades were good, and perhaps his approach rubbed off on me, because I went from getting Cs and Ds to getting Bs and Cs. I was slowly learning to channel my pent-up energy. Instead of being disruptive every chance that came my way, I was learning to pick my spots. I'll bet many hyper kids eventually learn to do the same, but at different ages.

My other salvation was my continued love of the outdoors, in particular a patch of swamp we called Pollywog Pond. Unlike the Meadows, which was several miles from our house, the marsh and woods around Pollywog Pond were within walking distance, perhaps a mile to a mile and a half from home. I absolutely loved that place, and while smoking cigarettes, drinking stolen beer, and having girlfriends was something I did to "fit in," visits to Pollywog Pond were just a natural extension of being a boy.

I recall my very first visit to Pollywog Pond when I was about ten years old, because it ended with me running halfway home. The area around Pollywog Pond was teaming with life, and in such variety that we never knew what we might encounter. To reach the pond itself, we had to follow a long trail that had a marsh on its left side, a stream on the right, and thickly forested hills beyond both the marsh and stream. Those slopes of oak, maple, and hemlock formed a small valley that was the perfect haven for wildlife. One friend called the area a "dingle," a word you never seem to hear anymore, but a perfect name for this small wooded dell. Sunlight dappled through the trees along the path, and the green, luxuriant vegetation grew so thick on either side you had the feeling it was growing rapidly enough that the trail might be choked with new growth by the time you retraced your steps.

If you were prone to claustrophobia, this was not the place to visit. It was the kind of valley you either loved or hated. I was in the former category, and the marsh looked inviting to me; pond lilies with their yellow flowers grew alongside tall and elegant cattails. A great blue heron, carefully stalking a fish or frog, was a wondrous sight, its patience something to marvel at. But a couple of friends I brought there couldn't wait to get out. To them the place was to be feared and avoided. They told me they felt they were being watched or, worse, stalked, and the strange birdcalls and rustling noises in the woods only fueled their fears. The vines that I would swing on were potential snakes, and if a young explorer wasn't watching their step, the coiled vines would trip them up and ensnare them. They couldn't understand how I could wade into the muck to above my ankles to get closer to something that caught my eye. The scent of rotting vegetation on sultry days disgusted them, and they viewed every insect as potentially venomous, every reptile as evil and aggressive. I never saw it that way. I simply viewed the place as somewhere to go and catch things. But on my very first visit, I felt like I was the "thing" ready to be caught.

I probably learned more about the creatures of New England in those acres than anywhere else. One day we might see great horned owls; the next, a muskrat, mink, or otter. It wasn't the mammals, however, that made the place special but the amphibians and reptiles—the sheer volume of which I have never seen again anywhere. There were hundreds of bullfrogs and leopard frogs, dozens of painted, snapping, and box turtles. And there were snakes sunning themselves right on the main pathway. These included garter, milk, and water snakes. They also included a snake I met on my very first trip because I stepped on it by accident. It was black and it was big—as thick around as my forearm and about four feet long. This was a black racer, a snake that feeds primarily on mice and when fully grown is near the top of the food chain at the swamps by Pollywog Pond.

I inadvertently stepped on the snake because I thought it was just a mud-encrusted tree branch off to the side of the trail where I had spotted a painted turtle. My foot landed on the black racer right in the middle of its body, and I remember being shocked to see the "branch" spring to life. As I hopped off the snake, its head reared up and attacked my leg. Thank God I had long pants on. The snake writhed around to take another jab at me. Mark and Greg were with me and heard my shriek, although I don't think they saw the snake. I just remember that as I screamed and started running, they were running right behind me, screaming themselves. It must have been quite a sight, because we didn't stop hollering and running until we reached Magnolia Circle, where we had stashed our bikes.

By the time we got home, the snake's size had grown to mythic proportions. I told my father it was as thick around as my thigh and longer than he was tall. I described its eyes as green and the serpent's tongue as a bright red. In reality, I didn't really see it clearly because I dashed out of the swamp like a greyhound. (Black racers can grow to almost six feet. One recently got tangled in my garden's strawberry netting, and it measured five feet even.)

It's a wonder we went back to Pollywog Pond after that scare, but being awed and occasionally frightened was part of its allure. Every trip there was filled with little adventures, and once we even saw another snake that looked as big as the one I stepped on. Sometimes we would go armed with homemade slingshots, which were incredibly accurate. We made the slingshots by cutting a sapling that had a V in it where branches forked from the main stem. Looking for a sapling with the perfect V was a wonderful way to spend a couple hours in the woods. My eyes searched for any sapling or branch of about an inch in diameter, scanning it for the perfect fork that would form a slingshot. (Indeed, even today I still can't help myself from examining the forest for "slingshot" trees.) This searching and subsequent construction of the weapon helped me learn about different trees. I quickly learned that a pine tree or hemlock was not stiff and sturdy enough for my purposes, and I began to understand the difference between softwoods and hardwoods.

Once the proper tree was located, the V, with the handle (the main branch) beneath it, was cut to proper size. Then we fashioned a piece of leather for the pocket, large enough to easily hold a marble-size rock. The leather was a two-inch rectangle, and two holes were punched on each side. Through these we secured small, thick rubber bands that we would loop together. The pocket would hang only three inches from the top of the V, but when we loaded the pocket with a rock and pulled back to take aim before firing, it stretched a good twelve inches. The force that those rubber bands created was formidable, and more than one frog went belly up when we scored a direct hit. Shooting frogs, chipmunks, and small birds was an incredibly stupid thing to do, but I think it's part of a young boy's DNA to want to hunt in some fashion, and it wasn't until I received a quality camera a couple years later that I substituted taking photos for taking life. Of all the activities I did in those younger days, killing frogs—or killing any living creature—and not eating the meat is the one I regret most.

Of the many days spent at Pollywog Pond, my favorite had nothing to do with snakes or frogs because it occurred in the winter of 1968 or 1969, when both reptiles and amphibians were deep in hibernation. I was with a neighbor named Rod, and we had hatched a plan to go ice fishing on the one-acre Pollywog Pond. I'm not even sure "pond" is the correct term, because it was really a big bulge in the stream where the water fanned out over a depression that was probably five feet deep. There was little current caused by the stream, which allowed the pond to ice over. In the springtime hundreds of inch-and-a-half-long pollywogs lay in the shallows along the shore; we once scooped a couple up, brought them home to our aquarium, and watched them slowly grow into frogs. They died before fully formed, so we abandoned that experiment.

We also knew there were fish in the pond, because we occasionally saw a small one jump. Our efforts to catch them in the summer were futile, so I bided my time until winter. On a bright and blustery Saturday morning, Rod and I walked down to the pond carrying a small backpack with fishing line, hooks, salami (for bait), a hammer, and a screwdriver. We didn't have an auger, so we figured we would simply chisel a hole through the ice with the tools we had. Of course our parents had no idea of what we were up to, but they rarely knew their children's exact whereabouts. My parents simply expected us to return home for lunch, home for dinner, and in the evening to be home at dark. We really had almost unlimited freedom, and that allowed us to learn in our own way, usually from trial and error. It fostered a wonderful sense of creativity and self-reliance. A good example is the slingshot: We were never shown how to make one, we simply kept experimenting until we got it right. We went on to make spears, bows and arrows, and even war clubs, and we managed never to hurt one another with any of them.

Like so many decisions made at that age, we rarely thought more than one step ahead, rarely looked before we leaped, and rarely considered the consequences of our actions. But we weren't stupid either, and a smidgeon of common sense helped keep us alive. We had no idea how thick the ice on the pond was, so Rod and I inched our way out. When the ice didn't crack or give way, we took that to mean it was perfectly safe, and we set up shop in the middle of the pond. Slamming the hammer down on the screwdriver caused shards of ice to fly in all directions. Every now and then the ice groaned and a hairline crack radiated out from the hole we were creating. It was a tedious process, but we took turns, and soon we were through the ice and to the water. We knew this because the screwdriver went right through my hand and sank to the bottom. Still, we cheered as if we had just struck oil.

The ice was not particularly thick, maybe two or three inches, but the two of us stood over the hole and played the age-old finger game of odds or evens to determine in what order we would hold the fishing line. Rod won, and we baited the hook with salami and dropped it down the hole. It wasn't long before he felt a little tug, but when he pulled up the line the salami was gone. At least we knew something was down there.

"Lower it just a foot down," I said to Rod, "then I want to look in the hole."

He did as I asked, and I lay on my belly with one eye directly over the opening. I cupped my hands around the hole so only a little light came through.

"I see fish!" I hollered. "One just took the salami!"

Peering through that little hole was a glimpse into another world. Five-inch fish darted about just a few inches from my head pressed to the ice. The fact that the pond was alive with life below the frigid ice seemed a miracle of sorts. I could not tell what kind of fish they were, but just seeing them glide through the water was enough to send adrenaline coursing through my body.

Rod took a piece of salami and told me he'd drop it down unhooked. I kept my eye next to the hole and moved my head just enough for him to release the salami.

"They took it!" I hollered. "As soon as you dropped it, they took it."

"I think our hook is too big for those little fish," said Rod.

"Yeah, that's right," I answered. "And maybe we're putting too much salami on the hook. They're just tugging it right off the hook."

"Let's try just baiting the hook with a tiny amount."

"It's my turn!"

"Just wait until I catch one, then you can have your turn," said Rod.

I reluctantly agreed.

Rod lowered his baited hook back down, and immediately a fish grabbed the salami; Rod gently pulled on the line. "I feel him! He's on the hook!"

The fish was pulled upward toward the hole, but instead of coming through the hole, it hit the side and tugged harder. Rod let some line out, fearing he'd lose the fish.

"Try bringing him up really slow this time," I said, "and let me watch as you do it."

I lay back down on the ice and pressed my face against the hole. I couldn't see a single fish. But as Rod slowly pulled the line in, the fish appeared, darting one way and then the other. I was mesmerized and could have watched that fish all day.

"Move your fat head!" screamed Rod.

I did, and Rod brought more line in at the same slow speed. Then the fish came through the hole and lay flopping on the ice.

"A trout!" I shouted.

It was a six-inch brook trout. Its back was marbled, red dots speckled its flanks, and its underside was a deep yellow-orange.

The two of us spontaneously shot to our feet and jumped, shouting, "We caught a trout!"

The ice answered us back with a sharp crack. We froze.

Now, for the first time, all my reading of adventure books did me some good. "Lie down!" I shouted.

I had read that if the ice starts to fracture, you should disperse your weight by lying down. I hit the ice and stretched out, but Rod was having none of it—he ran toward shore, and another crack rang out.

Rod made it safely to shore. I put the hammer in my backpack, grabbed the fishing line with the trout still flopping on its end, and followed Rod using a commando crawl, my stomach wiggling along the ice, looking very much like the fish I trailed behind.

I made it to shore, but I shudder to think how close we came to going through the ice and joining the screwdriver on the bottom of the pond. Rod and I, knowing we had dodged a bullet, exchanged sheepish smiles—and then forgot about our close call.

Rod decided to release the trout in the brook. After lying motionless for a moment, it slowly swam off into a tangle of roots, and we congratulated ourselves on our perceived virtue. We were simply happy to have proved to ourselves that we could catch a fish in the winter, and especially delighted to know that our little pond held trout.

That little Pollywog Pond, the fort, the Meadows, and other outdoor places helped keep me a bit grounded, connecting me to nature, which provided a welcome diversion to the peer pressure I felt at school as I began my teenage years. I'm convinced that had I not kept one foot in the woods during those formative years, I would have stayed on the path of nonstop detention and never have gone on to college.

⌒ ⌒

A professional fishing guide once asked me where I caught my first trout, and I explained that while it was my friend Rod who caught the brook trout at Pollywog Pond, that was the time I knew I was hooked. The guide went on to say that fishing brings out the little boy in all of us, telling me stories about stern-faced lawyers and doctors he'd take out on his boat morphing into whooping and laughing juveniles when they caught a big one. And he explained that when these same men lost a fish, they pouted like three-year-olds and took the failure personally.

I knew exactly what he meant, because I'm no different than those clients. In fact, I can remember trying to catch a fish all the way back to when I was six or seven years old, when I went angling in the basement of our home! Our basement had a drain of sorts: a three-foot-wide hole cut through the cement that led to an open pit extending about four feet into the earth below. Every now and then our basement flooded, and my father would remove the wooden covering over the hole and then, using a broom or a snow shovel, start pushing the water down this cavity. After one flooding he forgot to put the cover back on the hole, and I peered into its watery depths. I then ran into the garage, grabbed my fishing rod, scampered back into the basement, and dropped a lure into the hole. When I didn't catch anything, I put a bobber on the end of my line, then went outside and dug up a worm. My father asked me what I was doing, and I motioned for him to follow me back down into the basement. I pulled a crate over to the hole, sat down on the crate, and dropped my baited hook into the dark water, waiting for the bobber to be pulled under. I can't recall what my father might have said to me, but I do remember spending a half hour sitting by that drainage pit watching my bobber before I gave up. I later tried the same thing outside my house by the road, where a catch basin went down into a pipe. Today, little has changed. All water seems to tug at me, and it's all I can do to walk away and not make at least a couple casts. Norman Maclean was right; a river does run through it.

CHAPTER FOUR

THAT SAME WINTER WE CAUGHT THE TROUT AT POLLYWOG POND, I read a book that had a profound influence on my life and greatly fueled my desire to own a cabin. The book was not Thoreau's *Walden* or any other classic but a novel simply titled *The Pond*, by Robert Murphy. The story was about a boy named Joey who spends several weeks with his best friend at a cabin by a remote pond in Virginia in 1917. Together they fished for a granddaddy bass they had seen in the pond, hunted for squirrels and grouse, and befriended an old hunting dog named Charley. The book seemed to have been written just for me.

> *The woods around him, so silent and still, suddenly seemed to be full of a brooding mystery. . . . This was a feeling that he was going to have again and again when he was alone: a waiting and reaching-out to know and be merged with the mystery, an exaltation and a yearning. Many woodsmen have had it and are only completely happy when they are lost from the outside world and on the edge of it.*

The cabin Joey and his friend stayed at was primitive: no electricity, no running water, and a dilapidated outhouse. What it lacked in comforts was more than augmented by its location on the shore of a pond, where the boys observed otters, raccoons, mink, and the squirrels they hunted with rifles every chance they got. I too was squirrel hunting in 1968, although I didn't own a gun and probably never will. But hunting intrigued me—the stealth, the challenge, the rush of adrenaline when you found game. I'm sure it's the same for some other teenagers who spend considerable time outdoors, or, as Robert Murphy explained, some of us make the connection with our "primeval hunting ancestors." My homemade slingshot and bow and arrows were powerful enough to kill squirrels, rabbits, and birds if the shot was near perfect.

Strangely, capturing wildlife was just as exciting as killing it, and I did some illogical things. I remember I once shot two mourning doves, which tumbled out of the tree stunned but not seriously injured. I kept them in a cage and tried to nurse them back to health. One died, but the other recovered; I set it free, and felt exhilaration when it took wing to the sky. I know it makes little sense, especially since I'm the one who injured the bird in the first place, but nevertheless I gave myself a little pat on the back for helping the bird.

Another time I wanted my own squirrel for a pet. I'd located a squirrel's nest in the woods near our backyard, and decided the best way to have a pet squirrel was to capture one when it was young. (A friend of mine, Dale, had a pet squirrel; it would run to him and climb up on his shoulder whenever he whistled.) I thought the mission would be as simple as my shimmying up the tree, checking the nest for a young one, and grabbing it. Like so many of my plans, it lacked the depth of thought to consider variables that might cause me harm.

The tree was an oak, about forty feet in height, and the squirrel's nest was up near the top. Climbing the first two-thirds of the tree wasn't very difficult; there were plenty of branches for handholds and footholds. Up near the top, however, the slender trunk offered only a few branches that looked thick enough to support my weight, and it was slow going and more than a bit nerve-racking to be so high up. I inched my way closer to the nest, found a strong branch just beneath it, and rose up the last few inches. Just as my head was eye level with the nest, the unexpected happened. Out leaped a squirrel, passing just a couple inches from my head, startling and scaring me so much that for a moment I forgot where I was and leaned backward. My right hand slipped off the branch it had been clutching, and my feet slid off their perch. If not for my left hand staying firmly gripped on another branch, I would have tumbled almost forty feet to the ground. Instead, I swung back toward the main stem of the tree and wrapped myself around it with all my strength.

Now I was shaking, frightened both by the squirrel and by the potential fall. I hugged the tree, breathing heavily, knowing how lucky I was. But I soon rallied and thought to myself, *You've come this far; you might as well keep going.* That thought—those very words—have probably gotten more people killed in the outdoors than most any other notion. We humans are programmed to keep going whenever we've invested time and energy in an endeavor, no matter what our gut is telling us. My gut was literally shouting at me to get down off the damn tree, but my mind was saying, *Just one more minute.* I had only slipped a foot below the nest, so I climbed a bit higher and peered into the bowl-shaped layer of twigs. There were three baby squirrels in it, far younger than what I was hoping for. Still, I thought, *I'm here, I'm going to do it.* And so I grabbed one, tried to ignore its claws digging into my hand, put it inside my windbreaker, and started slowly down the tree.

I kept the baby squirrel in a cage on our porch. Into the cage I dumped a handful of acorns. When the squirrel didn't eat the acorns, I took peanuts from our kitchen and dropped those in as well. Still no response from the squirrel. What I didn't realize was that the squirrel was likely still nursing from its mother, and no amount or variety of nuts was going to induce it to eat. I gave the baby water, which it did drink, but in two days the squirrel was dead and I was heartbroken.

This strange relationship with animals—hunting some, "rescuing" others, and capturing them for pets—included just about every kind of creature I came across. Box turtles, painted turtles, snapping turtles, garter snakes, chipmunks, mice, and even a muskrat all fell victim to my illogical "love" of animals.

Maybe I can blame some of my actions on Willy Fitzpatrick and an incident back in the third grade. Our class had a pet rabbit named Nibbles, and each student was allowed to take care of Nibbles for a week. Children were selected to care for Nibbles when their name was pulled out of a hat, and I ached for my name to be one of the first. Instead my week was the very last one, right after Willy Fitzpatrick. In the days leading up to my week with Nibbles, I could barely contain my excitement and anticipation. The night before I was to be the caretaker, I selected the choicest carrots, celery, and lettuce—this rabbit and I were going to bond like no other mammalian team.

Imagine my surprise when I went into class the next day and there was no Nibbles. Its empty cage was there and so was Willy Fitzpatrick, but the rabbit was nowhere to be seen. I marched up to Mrs. Thatcher and asked where Nibbles was. She hesitated and then chose her words carefully. "I'm afraid I have bad news. Nibbles died the other night. I'm terribly sorry."

Reeling, I stepped back as if slapped in the face. Then the tears welled up. "What happened?" I asked, now sobbing.

Again, that hesitation from Mrs. Thatcher. "I guess it was just Nibbles's time to go. We will see about getting a hamster, and if we do, you'll be the first one to take it home."

I didn't want a stupid hamster. I wanted that beautiful white fluffy rabbit that all the other kids had a chance to take home. I was inconsolable. But at recess my sadness turned to rage. I asked Willy if he saw Nibbles die, and he answered, "No way; when I got home he was torn to shreds."

"What do you mean?"

"Don't you know?" he asked me. "Our dog ate Nibbles."

It took me a second to process this, and then I made a rush at Willy like an enraged bull. He sidestepped me and ran to Mrs. Thatcher, with me chasing after him.

"Michael Tougias," she said, standing in front of Willy, "you stop that right now. It was all a terrible accident, and no one is to blame."

But later I learned there was indeed a culprit, and his last name was Fitzpatrick. However it wasn't Willy but his older brother, Harry. Cogs, who was also in my class, is the one who put two and two together, and like a detective he laid out the sequence of events in a painstakingly clear dramatization so that there was no question of what had happened. Cogs told me that right off the bat he suspected Harry Fitzpatrick was involved. Apparently, just a few months earlier, Harry and Willy were playing at the Cogswells' house. While Willy and Cogs were out shooting baskets, Harry was in the house conducting an experiment. He had taken Cog's parakeet out of its cage and carried it into the kitchen, which happened to be the room where the family cat was dozing in the sun. Just then Mrs. Cogswell entered the kitchen. "Harry, what in the world are you doing?" she asked.

Harry just looked at her like it was the dumbest question he had ever heard. "I wanted to see what the cat would do to the bird."

Later Mrs. Cogswell explained what happened to Cogs, and said he was not allowed to play with the older Fitzpatrick boy.

And now, when Cogs learned of Nibbles' death, he got to thinking. *How did the Fitzpatrick's dog get Nibbles out of its cage?* The answer, of course, was that the dog had an accomplice: Harry. Once Cogs had figured this all out, he confronted Willy with his theory. "Willy," Cogs explained to me, "just lowered his head and looked at the ground. He didn't deny it and he wouldn't talk, so I knew that's exactly what happened."

Now, dear reader, I tell this story not only to vilify Harry Fitzpatrick (which I've been waiting fifty years to do) but also to show that I was only a step above him in the evolutionary chain. How could I—the boy who cried himself to sleep the night he learned of Nibbles's demise—just four years later go out and shoot a rabbit with his slingshot? It makes little sense, but this is what happened.

I was at the patch of woods where Mark, Greg, and I had our fort when I spotted a rabbit about twenty yards away. Of course I had my slingshot in my back pocket, and in my front pocket were a few marbles. I'd never killed a rabbit before, and had only hit one once, because they usually darted away in a zigzag manner whenever I approached. This particular rabbit didn't run, however, and went about its business munching on some grass. I couldn't resist the target. Loading a marble into the slingshot pouch, I took aim and shot. I was shocked when the rabbit keeled over, even more surprised when it didn't get up. The initial feeling I had over seeing the creature fall from a perfect shot was soon mixed with twinges of guilt as I walked to the rabbit, still expecting it to hop away, as if the finality of death wasn't real. Maybe I'd been watching too many Westerns on TV, where the killings seemed so sterile, but the rabbit was not like television. Blood was oozing out of the rabbit's head, and he wasn't going anywhere. (The marble had made a direct score on the rabbit's eye.) Death was no longer just an abstraction; it was right there in front of me, with the rabbit lying on its side. The image seemed to sear a spot in my soul, and I felt an acute sense of loneliness. Prior to shooting the rabbit, I'm sure I had some vague notion that if I ever actually killed one, I'd skin it for the pelt and then roast its meat over a fire. I did neither, and so the rabbit died strictly for my own sport.

I have no problem with people hunting who are going to utilize what they kill—only a vegetarian or vegan has the moral high ground to condemn the practice. But for me, the death of the rabbit by my slingshot began to sour me on the sport. My hunting didn't immediately stop; I still took an occasional potshot at a squirrel or bird, but I was passing up more and more opportunities. And incidents happened in the coming months that further pushed me away from my trusty slingshot.

During that summer of 1968, according to my diary (which I still have), my cat caught a rabbit and brought its lifeless body back to our house. I was a bit disgusted with our cat, knowing it certainly didn't need to kill the cottontail for food, conveniently overlooking the fact that I had done the exact same thing. I examined the rabbit closely, and although it had no major wounds, it didn't seem to be breathing and appeared dead. Scooping it up in a shovel, I carried it to the far corner of our backyard, where I dug a grave for it. I put the rabbit in the hole and threw a couple spades of dirt over it. Then the most amazing thing happened. Like Lazarus, the rabbit suddenly scrambled to its feet, leaped out of the hole, and crashed right into my leg. I yelped, dropped the shovel, and ran, thinking the rabbit was attacking me. I looked over my shoulder just in time to see the cottontail streaking off into the woods.

Of course the rabbit had never died at all, but must have been in some shock-induced state of near death. When the shovelfuls of dirt landed on it, perhaps that helped snap it back to consciousness, and off it went. The whole incident gave me pause—I was delighted that this rabbit beat the odds and would run free again. Slowly it was sinking into my thick head that I'd rather see a live rabbit racing away than a dead one as still as a stone. Wild rabbits, Nibbles, squirrels; they all taught me life was fragile and there are no guarantees.

As if to drive the lesson home, an event happened that summer I'll never forget. In front of our house was a large pine tree whose roots were growing under our tar driveway, cracking the asphalt. My father and a neighbor decided to chop it down, each taking turns with an ax. While my neighbor was using the ax, he must have struck the tree incorrectly, because the ax-head came flying free of the handle and embedded itself in my father's calf. Blood came gushing out, and while my neighbor called for an ambulance, my father used his shirt to try and staunch the bleeding. Luckily, the ax-head did not hit a major artery or my father might have died—especially in the days before 911 and paramedics.

Still, it was a major wound, and I remember almost fainting when I saw it. Incredibly, my father took just one day off from work at the bakery. He went to work as if nothing happened, but he was limping for a good two weeks. That guy was as tough as nails. He wasn't the biggest or the strongest, but this incident and many more to come showed me he had incredible willpower and endurance. He never complained about that wound, and joked that it was all his fault: "This dumb Greek was standing way too close to a swinging ax. I'm lucky it didn't hit me in the head." Then he added, "If it did hit me in the head, maybe it would have worked out just fine and taken away some of my big nose!"

I remember my dad telling me that not only was he fortunate he wasn't killed from the accident, but equally important—at least in his mind—was that he wasn't maimed. A severe or permanent injury, he explained, would mean he couldn't work and would entail multiple medical bills. We, like most people of that time, had no disability or medical insurance, and being unable to work meant no pay. I can remember Dad saying what a fine line there is between the good life we were able to live and catastrophe, and how if the ax-head's trajectory had been just a half inch to the right, he might not have made it.

Eight years later our family was not to be so lucky during another freak accident.

———

Thinking back on the ax incident, I realize I can't remember a single time my father complained about anything in his personal life. (I don't call his anger toward me complaining; that was simply his frustration at me for not listening to him or my mother.) In fact, my father was one of the happiest people around. He was content with his bakery job, loved his family, and had a passion for his two hobbies of history and people. That's right, one of his hobbies was people. He had more friends than I could count, and they were always coming to the house for a drink. They ranged from his bakery workers such as eighteen-year-old Bob Potter to old Albert, the rough-and-tumble French Canadian who was in charge of the bread mixer. And then there were the church ladies, the aunts and uncles, his friends from elementary school, his barber, his car mechanic, a bartender, his bookie, the local cops, and on and on. All of them visited the house. All of them received at least one martini. And all of them got the tour of Dad's history book collection, which was massive. They included rare books such as *Glimpses of the World*, published in 1892, to just about every book written on World War II, the Civil War, and the Revolutionary War, including his favorite, *Now We Are Enemies*. And his books on King Philip's War and the French and Indian War surely sparked my desire to later write my own books on those subjects.

Hundreds of books lined our den, and on almost every page my father either underlined passages he liked or stuck in a piece of paper with his own thoughts. His passion for history knew no bounds, and I remember one year he devoted his only day off from work, a Saturday, to join a group of Revolutionary War reenactors. He shocked the whole family when he came home from the first meeting and stepped out of his car dressed in buckled black leather shoes, white stockings that went to his knees, rough cloth breeches, giant black belt, white linen shirt, wool coat, and black tricorn hat. I remember a part of me wanted to laugh and another part was in awe. Then he went to the trunk of the car and pulled out this enormous musket, powder horn, and cartridge box. We all talked at once. My mother cried out in a pained voice, "Aaaaarrrrtttttt, you can't bring that gun in the house!" while I shouted, "Let me shoot that gun! I promise just one shot!"

My father ignored us. Instead he put the musket over his shoulder and marched up the driveway, around the side of the house, and into the backyard, where he knelt down in the firing position as if the Kimmels' house behind ours was hiding the whole British Army.

"Aaaarrrtttt," my mother wailed, "the neighbors!" It was a familiar cry. And it made me happy. It meant that I wasn't the only one driving her crazy. While I caused her grief by letting snakes loose in the house, trying to sleep with Jane, and other infractions, I think my dad did the same. As outgoing and gregarious as he was, my mother was the opposite, quiet and reserved. She craved peace and quiet, and I'm certain she would have preferred fewer visitors coming to the house at Art's insistence. And I know she wasn't happy when my father and friends sometimes got hammered on martinis, which he called "whacking down a few." If any of the visitors were female, my father would get the stereo or radio cranked up and soon he'd be dancing with them. The man was a dancing machine, and he was in the habit of singing along with the music, absolutely butchering the songs. My sister, Lynn, had turned him on to the Beatles, and he especially loved their slower love songs, where he could slow dance and croon at the same time, his high notes sounding as if they came from a beagle.

Of course I was embarrassed by all his theatrics, just as my mother was. But a funny thing happened when I grew up—I would egg him on because I loved the sheer joy he infused into any get-together. And when I had kids of my own, they would sing and dance with him, even listen to his history stories and marvel at his musket and powder horn.

I wish I had kept a photo of my father in his Revolutionary War uniform because he loved it so. Many years later, when he was eighty-one years old, he walked into his favorite bar on Halloween dressed in the uniform. Waitresses hugged and kissed him, but the manager politely told him he had to put the musket back in his car before he could have his first drink.

—◠—

Somewhere in the course of 1968, I felt I was outgrowing the Pollywog Pond, the woods around our fort, and even the Meadows. A friend of the family, Mr. Bob Guilmette, took me trout fishing with his son Gary in the hilly part of Massachusetts called the Berkshires. It was my first real exposure to a clear, rushing river that coursed around boulders and through hemlock-shaded chasms. Although we didn't catch a single fish, I saw several trout in one deep pool, and I would have given anything to have brought a mask and snorkel so I could dive down and be among them. That trip opened my eyes to a different kind of environment than the slow-moving streams and rivers I was familiar with. Rushing water held an almost magical power over me, and still does to this day. The more wild the river, the more I seem to enjoy it.

These rivers are perfect habitat for trout, and that particular river in the Berkshires seemed to crystallize what I was looking for. The cleanest, coldest, fastest rivers flowed down off mountains, and I soon equated hill country with the type of river I loved best and the landscape where I felt most at home. I'd grown up in the valley along the Connecticut River where white pine, oak, and swamp maple were the primary trees, but in the higher elevations, such as the Berkshires, grew towering stands of white birch, hemlock, beech, and spruce, and those trees seemed to have a stronger pull on me. Maybe that was yet another reason I looked forward so much to our family trips to Vermont—it may have been the power of those trees as much as the mountains.

Before I knew this type of river existed, my plan for a cabin never had a specific setting. But now there was absolutely no doubt; my cabin had to be in the mountains and far from developed areas. Joey's cabin in the hills of Virginia only reinforced the notion that to have the most adventures you had to be far from other people, with plenty of forest to explore. Maybe that's why I read *The Pond* three times in 1968.

CHAPTER FIVE

EVEN THOUGH I HAD LOTS OF FRIENDS, I WAS ALSO SOMETHING OF A loner. There weren't many kids riding their bikes to the library and coming back with an armload of books. I must have inherited the love of books from my father, who often said, "A man's best friend is his library. I don't know what I'd do without my books." I could not have agreed more. Every book I read resulted in a "review card" summary of the story, how I felt about it, and finally my own rating system from "awful" rising up to "most excellent." Here's a compelling review for *Tomahawk Shadow*: "Bart, after an escape from his old man, found Wandering Bird's village. They lived happily ever after. (VG; Very Good)." And to think later in life, I did reviews for *Publishers Weekly*.

But those small volumes I digested had an effect. I read everything I could about Native Americans, and one of the very first books I later had published was *Until I Have No Country: A Novel of King Philip's Indian War*. The romance I wove into that story must have come from reading books such as *Savage Gentleman*, on which my review card zeroed in on the implied sex. "Jeff was taken captive, but all he cared about was the tantalizing Indian woman. VE; Very Excellent." I guess Jeff must have been one tough dude to be taken captive by Indians but only care about a hottie.

Spawning my cabin interest was *The Lost Wagon*, in which my review said, "Joe Tower wanted to go west where the land would be his own. He had Indian fights, parties, blizzard dangers, and heartbreak. But once in Oregon things were better. VE: Very Excellent." And of course when you are young, you know what you want to do before society brainwashes you, and I read many books like *Wilderness Warden*, which I gave a high rating and said, "Dan's joy of the woods and camping in snowstorms ended when he must capture a poacher. He did, and became a warden."

If all of us kept these review cards, diaries, or letters from childhood and looked at them when we turned twenty-one, we'd get a glimpse into our future, or at least a reminder of our pure self and our true interests. As a young teenager I was not only smitten with tales of the forests but also with survival-at-sea stories, which later became the focus of six books I wrote. For example, at age thirteen I read *Men Against the Sea* and gave it an "Excellent" rating, even though my review focuses on the irrelevant: "This is the story of traveling 3,000 miles in a small boat after Captain Bligh and his followers were cast from the mutinous *Bounty*. For 41 days they didn't even go to the bathroom." Amazing the things you can learn. (I'm going to have to reread that book and see if that is true. If it is, I'm going to figure out their trick for a better night's sleep.)

Of course any mention of fishing in a book automatically garnered high marks, and authors such as Jim Kjelgaard usually got my VE rating. For his book *Stormy* I wrote: "The catching of a four-foot pike added to the story." That was the extent of my summary, but I'm sure the book had characters and a plot. Fishing even caught my eye in *One Flew Over the Cuckoo's Nest*: "McMurphy came into the nut house and brought girls and booze. But it was the fishing trip that opened up the patients." Deep analysis there, when a young reviewer realizes angling for fish, rather than wine and women, can lead to psychological healing. I didn't mention Nurse Ratched but of course wrote that the Chief was "really cool. We would be friends."

I did read some classics, such as *Of Mice and Men*, but my review only said, "Lennie murdered a <u>tart</u>, and shattered Lennie and George's dream of owning a farm." I don't know why I underlined the word "tart" in the review, but at least I gave it a "G" for good. I did, however, know the formula for success, summing up *The Godfather* with a simple "filled with violence, sex, and action." My worst rating was for *Macbeth*, which received an "AW" for awful, and I didn't bother to write even one line of commentary. A close runner-up, which garnered a "Poor," was *The Scarlet Letter*. Maybe that had something to do with the last two lines in my review: "Daughter Pearl is an Elf. This is a book about dumb Puritan Life." So what book got the coveted "Most Excellent Rating"? Well, here I showed good taste, and the book I chose is still my favorite: *To Kill a Mockingbird*.

Two novels about the outdoors received high marks and stand out in my memory because they influenced my quest for the cabin and yearning for adventure. *Cache Lake Country* had me hooked from the first page, which featured a map of lakes, rivers, mountains, and the location of a cabin. I recently reread the book, and I fully understood its appeal, with lines seemingly written specifically for me: "Then as the sun cleared the hills and turned the still black water into gold, I remembered. This was the lake of my boyhood dreams. . . . I knew then that I found the place I had always wanted to be." The book featured an outdoorsman named Jim, befriended by an Indian who teaches him the fine points of living in a remote area, and how even the water and trees have a spirit. I remember not just reading the book but studying how the two men lived off the land, built a canoe, and trapped beaver. At the end of *Cache Lake Country* there is even a Woodcraft Index, which helps you locate the pages on the use of a compass, the formation of a dewdrop, and even the care of your feet! If I put as much time into my schoolwork as I did absorbing that book and visualizing the adventures in it, I'd be a straight-A student. Some of the information stayed with me for years—whether consciously or not—especially the location of the cabin, which was high on a knoll where Jim could look out across the lake to distant mountains. That sounded perfect. And so I drew a map with a winding trail up a ridge that led to the cabin I someday hoped to buy. On my map the cabin looked down on a pond ringed by a mountain range. I drew in a brook, an orchard, and even an outhouse. It's remarkable how a visual image can help you attain a goal.

Farley Mowat's *Lost in the Barrens* was the other book I still remember after all these years. It was a tale of survival and had a particularly gripping whitewater river adventure that prompted me to make my first major purchase in life: a two-man raft. My parents thought I was crazy, and it turned out they were right, because that raft caused me to come within a whisker of losing my life. When a book can make a kid go out and spend all his money, the writing must be damn good, and it was. I literally thirsted after fast-paced books and spent hours at the library hunting them down. None of my friends knew of my passion, and I certainly tried to keep it a secret, but I can't help but think of all the joys good books have brought me over the years, and wonder if kids today still ride their bikes to the library to be transported to places like Cache Lake Country or the Arctic Barrens.

Other interests were equally unusual for that age, and one was growing a vegetable garden. Opie's neighbor Henry had a garden that covered his entire backyard, almost half an acre, and each time I was at Opie's house, I made it a point to walk through this wonderful world of greenery and fresh food. Rows of corn, tomatoes, squash, peppers, carrots, green beans, you name it. Some of the plants were so tall that walking down the path felt like going through a magical tunnel in different hues of green. Henry was probably fifty years old and didn't mind my wandering his garden. He would come out and point out the crops that were going great guns and those that "needed work." It was such an eye-opener for me because my father didn't have a green thumb, and my mom was strictly an indoor person, her biggest foray into our yard being a trip to the clothesline. Consequently, our backyard looked like most others: a monoculture of grass shaded by oaks.

The need to grow things was in me long before I made regular wistful visits to Henry's garden. As early as ten or eleven years old, I asked my mother to buy me seeds for my favorite vegetable: corn. The stalks grew about two and half feet high and never produced any ears. I didn't know that they needed to cross-pollinate, and I had planted just two short rows rather than a "box" of plants at least seven feet by seven feet. The next year I planted a few tomato seedlings, but they grew into wispy, scrawny things that might have yielded one or two green tomatoes in late September.

Maybe my desire to grow a garden had something to do with how good some of the food from Henry's garden tasted. Opie and I often had raw snow peas, or his mother would steam squash or sauté zucchini. That form of cooking was a revelation to me. In the 1960s most people, my mom included, were boiling vegetables into a soggy unrecognizable goop. The fiber, the taste, the very vitamins inherent in the plant were stripped away by the boiling water, and what was left usually made me gag. And the Tougias family food came from the supermarket, where in those days produce might have been sitting on the shelf for a few days. But I'd been to the promised land at Henry's. I knew what a locally grown tomato, cucumber, or radish tasted like, and I wanted some of my own.

Observing Henry's garden finally made me put two and two together: Plants need sun. The garden plot my father allowed me to dig in was in the shade. The next year I changed locations, added some cow manure, and lo and behold I had tomatoes, radishes, carrots, zucchini, yellow squash, and more. That success launched a lifetime of vegetable gardening, and, like books, the act of growing things was as natural to me as breathing. I'd feel an enormous void if I couldn't do either.

Perhaps the best consequence of my vegetable garden was my father's reaction. He had just come home from work and was walking from the driveway around to the back door when I saw him. I intercepted him and handed him a tomato. It being a hot and humid day, I could smell the sweat on him—at the bakery it must have been well over a hundred degrees working by the industrial-size ovens. He looked exhausted, like he'd just gone ten rounds in a boxing ring. Following him into the house, I remember him cutting the tomato in half, sprinkling salt on it, and taking an enormous bite. Juice dripped down his chin onto the white T-shirt. Then he smiled. "There is nothing like a homegrown tomato," he exclaimed. "This is fantastic."

Handing me the other half of the tomato, he said, "*Mangia, mangia.*"

Maybe I was wrong about my father not liking me. Maybe he saw some redeeming qualities that might someday offset the trouble I brought his way.

To finance my hobbies of fishing, gardening, and what I hoped would be future rafting trips, I bought a paper route. Yes, *bought*. A paper route was a profitable business, and paperboys or girls didn't just give away an established business when they were ready to move on; they sold it to the highest bidder. Of course I wanted the route closest to my house because delivery would be done by bicycle, so I told the current paperboy, Howie Gershwitz, that when he was ready to sell, talk to me first.

Looking back, the entire paper route experience was an incredible lesson in what it takes to be an entrepreneur. First you had to find the business you might be good at, then you had to save or secure the funds to get started, and finally you had to work your ass off to make a profit. Step one for me was negotiating with Howie, who drove a hard bargain by first saying he wasn't interested in selling but adding that if he did ever sell, the price would be fifty dollars.

That was a lot of money for a forty-home route. I asked my father about it, and he said it all sounded good, probably thinking that anything constructive that occupied my time would keep me from manufacturing strife. Then I asked my sister, Lynn, who had three years of babysitting experience, if the price sounded right. She counseled me never to pay full price, and that Howie was a blowhard. Next I called Opie, who in turn asked an older kid in his neighborhood what he paid for his paper route. Opie reported back that I should pay no more than thirty dollars; that was the going rate for a medium-size route.

I wanted to be a paperboy badly, and Howie had picked up on that, coupled with my lack of negotiation experience. When I told him I only had thirty dollars, he laughed, saying, "Your father owns a bakery; get the money from him." I tried to explain that being a baker wasn't like owning a furniture store, supermarket, or car dealership. "Bakers don't make much money," I said, "so I gotta pay for this myself." He gave a breezy high-pitched laugh, lifted his considerable bulk onto his bike, and without looking at me said, "Tootles."

I figured I was finished, but a week later Howie was back, and his price had dropped to forty dollars. A light bulb went off in my thick little head. *He has no other interested buyers.* I stuck to my thirty dollars. Once again he ended the conversation with his strange laugh, mounted his bike, and then patted the big canvas bag of newspapers hanging from his shoulders, saying, "Too bad; you might have been able to do the job."

The next day I waited for him making the rounds. When he wheeled into our driveway I simply said, "thirty-five dollars." He said "done," and we shook hands. Then I went into the house and extracted the money from my piggy bank. (I really did have one—it was green with a sketch of a woman on the side of the bank holding a bag of money.) Counting out thirty-five dollars was painful. At least when I bought the raft, I knew it would lead to fun and excitement. Whereas the paper route meant responsibility, and the payment of thirty-five dollars pretty much wiped out what I had in the piggy bank. I had a real bank account, but my father drilled it into my head that I'd need that for books in college, knowing I was eyeing that money for a cabin.

Buying the paper route was easier than delivering, and a heck of a lot more straightforward than "collecting" when it was time for customers to pay their monthly bill. Some customers literally hid on me when I rode up on my bike and knocked on the door. Others said to come back because they either had no cash or only large bills. I'd say I can make change or a check would be fine, and they'd just say, "come back tomorrow." And of course the next day no one would be home.

The biggest obstacle to distributing the papers was a dog named Fury. Now this was no ordinary run-of-the-mill aggressive dog. This was a vicious demon housed in the body of a Great Dane. How and why my parents even let me deliver papers to that dog's residence is a mystery to me still. They knew about Fury, had seen the thing with their own eyes, but maybe because they had never been chased by it, they didn't understand the terror.

The first time I delivered to Fury's home, the dog was inside. I could hear its deep guttural bark, and as I approached the front steps, I realized all that separated me from the beast was a glass storm door. The dog's back came up to my chest, and I swear the top of his head was the same height as mine. With a coat of jet-black fur and drool coming out of its mouth, this snarling mass of muscle must have weighed close to one hundred pounds, which would have made it ten pounds heavier than me. This was the closest I'd ever been to the monster, and my legs felt like jelly and my mouth went dry. I laid the paper on the front landing and backed away, not daring to take my eyes off the dog. Right then and there I vowed that I'd never go to that door again, but instead throw the paper onto the driveway without ever stopping my bicycle.

For the first month that plan served me well. Fury would see me coming, let out these god-awful *Wooooofffffs*, and froth at the mouth behind the storm door. Day after day this went on, and I hardly gave the dog another thought. Then it happened. I should have known something was up when I didn't hear Fury barking in the house. Instead, just after I flung the paper, something big and black caught my eye coming at me from around the far side of the house. Fury was loose!

He was running at me like a race horse, and he looked as big as one the way he galloped over the yard. I tried to scream, but nothing came out. I was on my bike with a newspaper bag draped over one shoulder and two baskets on the rear of the bike carrying more papers. Adrenaline coursed through me and my legs pumped with a purpose, but carrying the weight of the newspapers made the bike's tires seem like they were in quicksand. Luckily, I never stopped riding when I first threw the paper at Fury's house, so I had a bit of momentum. But when I glanced back it was clear the dog was gaining on me, and I shook, panic-stricken. I made it about forty feet down the street to the house next to Fury's and looked back again. I didn't have to look far; the dog's head was about five feet behind me and waist-high, with little spits of white drool flying off its tongue. I literally felt the fear zip up my spine to the back of my neck. I was a goner.

"Fury!" someone bellowed. It wasn't the brute's owner but a neighbor out raking leaves. The dog turned its head then wheeled around, and I made good my escape. I glanced over my shoulder and saw Fury trotting back to his house.

I told my father and mother about the incident, but I don't believe they ever did anything about it. They were respectful of neighbors to a fault, reluctant to call the owner of Fury and complain. Instead they said it was the first time this had happened and the dog had never been loose before. I was livid that my father didn't take action, and snapped, "Well, I guess I'll just let the dog kill me." He wasn't amused. My mother said something to the effect that maybe I was too young for a paper route, and the next thing I knew my parents were in a big fight. A big fight in which I'm sure my father viewed me as the instigator.

So I had to deal with the problem on my own, living in dread every time I had to go to Fury's house. I did alter my method of delivery, however. In the past I had slowed at the driveway and even made a little U-turn up it before carefully throwing the folded paper. But after almost becoming dinner for the dog, I changed tactics so that I was literally flying by the house and, without slowing down, pitching the paper up the driveway.

Fury never came after me again, but its owners had the gall to complain to the paper company that their newspaper was found either at the end of the driveway or on the grass. The company policy at the time was to insert the paper in the person's front door or leave it partially under the front mat (incredibly, the papers were not wrapped in plastic). I was reprimanded by the company. I told my mother about it, and she shocked me by taking my side, saying, "Just keep doing what you're doing. If those neighbors complain again, I'll call them." This from the most reserved, mild-mannered, polite, never-make-waves woman on the planet. Her stance had me absolutely floored, and I knew then and there my mom loved me. She had never told me that, and I had always wondered, but for her to say she'd stand up for me against the neighbors was an act of courage because it was so contrary to her nature.

Delivering papers was a big commitment. I had to be home at 4:00 p.m. when they arrived to get them to my customers right away, rain or shine. Sunday papers were brutal, because first I'd have to assemble two different sections into one, and they were too thick to fold into thirds like I did with the daily papers. Back then, before the internet took the business away, the classified advertisements alone covered more pages than the news did. Of course the entire paper weighed a ton, and the most I could carry on my bike was about fifteen Sunday papers, requiring me to return home to get more after delivering those.

The weight of those Sunday papers caused a close call one icy winter morning. I was on my bike coming around a bend in the road, and a car was traveling in my direction. I put on the brakes to slow the bike, and that caused me to go into a skid. The bike fell on top of me, pinning me in the middle of the road. The driver of the car—I can still clearly see her wide eyes—hit the brakes, and she too went into a skid. The car kept coming, and I saw the woman open her mouth, probably screaming, just before the car was going to run me over. I was literally a foot or two from the front grill when the car came to a stop. The shaken woman got out and helped pull my bike off me, saying over and over, "I'm so sorry, I couldn't stop." I muttered, "It wasn't your fault," but I never looked at her. I just wanted her to leave. As soon as she got back in her car and pulled away, the tears came. Then I gathered my papers, walked my bike around the bend, and delivered my entire route on foot.

Still, the paper route was one of the best experiences of my boyhood in terms of kicking some maturity into me. It's probably wishful thinking, but I wish kids today were encouraged to have similar jobs long before they get their driver's license.

CHAPTER SIX

THERE IS A PLEASANT ANTICIPATION AND MYSTERY WHEN YOU EMBARK on a journey and don't know exactly where you are going. That was how I felt when thirty other campers and I set out on an overnight backpacking trip. We were members of an overnight camp in the Berkshires, and our counselors equipped us with ancient canvas army surplus packs to carry our sleeping bags, tarps, and food for a two-day hike to parts unknown. The summer camp was my first extended stay away from home, and while I was initially nervous, that soon evaporated as I made new friends and got to do fun stuff like shooting .22 caliber rifles at the rifle range, staying up half the night talking, and taking out rowboats for fishing. But this particular hike is what I remember most because it didn't go as planned. (Aren't those the experiences we all remember most clearly? Bad trips get seared into our soul, followed by exceptionally adventurous ones, and the rest get washed away by time because nothing unusual happened.)

I volunteered for the trip because my cabin counselor Ed Kellogg, who was seventeen years old, was also going, and he was such a cool dude I would have followed him through fire. Ed had just the right leadership skills for the eight kids in his cabin: He was there if we needed him, but let us be kids if we didn't. In other words, we were free from being told what to do every second of the day. While we had structured time such as softball games, boating, or duty in the mess hall, there was more than enough downtime to go fishing in the camp's lake or simply lie down on our bunks during the heat of the day and talk or play cards. And at night we often gathered around a campfire and told stories. Ed's favorite tale was about a camper from years gone by who broke the rules and went out on the lake alone at night in a canoe. Bad mistake. He was attacked by a six-foot frog. The frog was said to have rammed the canoe, spilling the camper into the water, where the frog made a snack out of him. Although I knew the story couldn't be true, another part of me thought *maybe* . . . . Ed was that good a storyteller.

Eight boys from all over western Massachusetts were assigned to Ed's cabin. I especially remember one overweight red-haired kid who we nicknamed Bubbles. He could easily have been bullied or picked on, but that never happened. While we poked fun at him, it was always good-natured, and that was because of our wise seventeen-year-old counselor. Ed had a special knack for making the eight campers feel like a team, and Bubbles was part of that team. I remember Ed saying, "You guys are the best bunkhouse in the camp. You treat each other like brothers." We didn't at first, but because Ed would repeat that mantra—and we all looked up to Ed—we soon became like brothers. Whatever they paid Ed and the other counselors, it wasn't enough. They were in a position to influence our lives just as much as a schoolteacher, maybe more, because they were just a handful of years older.

I always wondered what happened to Ed, and I worried that he got drafted into the army and shipped to Vietnam. The war was raging, and once a young man turned eighteen with a low draft number and no college deferment, the military came calling. Unless you had a rich daddy who could pull a few strings, a person like Ed might find himself hunkering for cover in a rice paddy instead of leading hikes in the Berkshires.

Anyway, the hike that I remember got off to a bad start, because after just two miles of "marching," most of us were pooped from lugging our overstuffed canvas packs on a hot summer day. We all wore blue jeans because we'd been warned we'd be passing through poison ivy and brush. The line of campers was stretched out over a quarter of a mile, and all of us were complaining of the heat, blisters, and hunger (we hadn't eaten in two whole hours). The counselors, who were high school kids not much older than us, told us we were big babies and to act like men. We responded that we weren't men and that a forced march was not what we signed up to do.

One of the counselors got us to pick up our pace a little bit by promising that we would soon have a chance to cool off. I interpreted that to mean we would have a chance to rest and take a swim. But after another couple miles of hiking, we came to a river, and I realized we would be wading across it. I was pumped: This is what the explorers in *Cache Lake Country* did! The only thing better would have been if we were on horseback and could ride across.

It had been a rainy summer and the river was running strong, but without a moment's hesitation the lead counselor entered the water. He uncoiled a rope then addressed the gathered campers on shore, explaining that we were to follow him in single file and hold onto the rope. We should take our sneakers off and put them in our packs and keep close together along the rope. Two of the other counselor would be mixed in with the campers, and two more would be bringing up the rear if anyone needed help. He asked if there were any questions and, when there were none, told us to "stay close together and come on in, the water's fine." We all charged in at once.

The water was only knee-deep near the shore, but the rocks on the bottom were slick. With the heavy pack on my back, I halted my charge and picked my way along. I found holding the rope actually made my balance less steady, so I let go and spread my arms as if I were on a sky-high tightrope. I loved the challenge, feeling like John Colter of the Lewis and Clark Expedition fording the Yellowstone on his way to the Rockies.

That positive energy left me and every other camper when we got to the middle of the river and the current knocked us down like bowling pins. I grabbed the rope, but not before my pack was submerged. Somehow my bathing suit came free of the pack, and I watched it whisked away by the river. The water was up to my waist, and I was frozen in mid-river, watching the carnage around me.

Several kids who fell couldn't get back on their feet. Their wet blue jeans made their legs heavy, and the big packs pinned them down. The packs made the ones who landed on their stomachs look like swimming turtles; the ones who landed on their backs looked like overturned turtles, their legs and arms flailing and sticking up from their shells below the waterline. Counselors reached out and grabbed the ones they could, but three campers were carried downstream, shouting for help.

One counselor, who wore a patch over his eye, swam after them and somehow corralled two out of the three runaway campers and brought them back to the rope. But he missed one kid, and I watched in horror as the current took him downstream, with only his bobbing pack visible. We campers all shouted useless words of encouragement, as if we were wishing someone well before they embarked on a cruise. Luckily, the eye patch counselor started swimming after him.

It seemed to take us forever to get to the other side of the river. Every time a camper slipped and fell into the water, he took one or two others with him. When we reached the shore, we all collapsed. The eye patch counselor was there with the kid who got swept away. There is no doubt in my mind that the counselor saved his life. The camper was traumatized but recovered quickly, although his pack was sacrificed in the rescue.

All of us had wet sleeping bags and clothing, and I wondered how we would ever get through the night. But no one talked about that. Rather each camper wanted to tell the story of how he almost drowned. The counselors, on the other hand, went off into a group to talk privately. Whatever they talked about, they did not abort the trip but instead gave us a pep talk about how we were almost at our camping spot near the Knightsville Dam.

How do I remember all this? Partly from saved letters and postcards I wrote to family members. Here is what the letter on the river disaster says in its original form:

Finally we came to a river. So we started crossing it. What a mistake. It was up to our waist, sometimes higher. The current pushed us. We were waited down by our packs. It was hard to stand and every one was falling. I fell in and got my sleeping bag and all my close wet. My bathing suit fell out and I couldn't save it. It was my good one. I cut my foot. I never had such an adventure. Kids were swimming and trying to get to land. One kid almost drowned. I'M NOT EXAG-SURERATING. PS: I hope you have been taking care of my garden.

Yes, my mother kept my letters and postcards, and she saved them for me, knowing I'm a pack rat, or "historian." Here is a sampling of some of the postcards I wrote:

Dear Mom, say hello to Dad. Right often.

Dear Mom and Dad, we through an egg at another cabin. We got killed.

Dear Mom, will you be coming to visit? If you do bring underwear and candy.

Dear Bob, we are going fishing tonight. We took a pound of bread from the mess hall. Water my garden.

Dear Mark and Lynn, We go to bed at 9:30 but don't get to sleep until 12. We have neat discutions.

Dear Mom and Dad, my cousilor is nice. He always plays records. I wrote my name all over the walls. How is my garden?

Dear Mom, I'm getting results from my bicycle crash at home a few days ago. My sides are ripped and killing me. I can't even make it to my bunk without help. But I'm having a lot of fun. Bring candy. Take care of my garden.

Later in life, when I had a son of my own, I sent him to camp knowing he would love it and have adventures like I did. I saved his letters:

Camp is bad. The food is bad. They make us play games that stink. Counselors are really mean. Can't wait till it's over.

———

I feel the same about the camp experience as I do about the paper route—they are important to a young boy's maturation. But so many of today's overnight camps are specialized: computer camp, tennis camp, swimming camp, and on and on. I'll bet they are a product of what the parents think their children should be doing rather than what the children really want to do. Tommy's going to be the next Bill Gates, Timmy the next Andre Agassi, and Willy the next Michael Phelps. But I suspect young boys and girls want fun, adventure, and new experiences rather than a grind in an effort to become an elite specialist.

Protective parenting is also responsible. Precious Timmy can't sleep under the stars in a wet sleeping bag; he'll get pneumonia and die. Yet somehow I survived that night at the Knightsville Dam, and looking back I think it toughened me up. But today's parents don't care about lessons in overcoming adversity, unless of course it's related to helping pad their child's accomplishments to get into college or land a scholarship. So woodcraft, paddling a canoe, reading a compass, and building a fire are pushed to the side as "useless." No wonder I see so many children of today's era afraid of the woods, afraid of the dark, afraid of any body of water that isn't a swimming pool. Yes, maybe they can program a computer and excel at a sport, but did they hear the call of a loon or the yipping of coyotes at night or spot a shooting star?

Psychologists call our children's disconnect with the outdoors "nature deficient disorder," but I call it "afraid of the woods." Being fearful while in the woods or on the water means they will stay indoors, and those kids are missing something they will probably never grow accustomed to. I have no doubt they are forgoing a *spiritual* joy that can only come from being free and comfortable to explore the forests, rivers, mountains, and lakes.

—◆—

While camp toughened me up, it only marginally improved my decision making. When I returned home, I was up to my old tricks.

CHAPTER SEVEN

My dad didn't know what headache I'd cause him next, but he was still my dad, and Mark and I would pester him to take us fishing. The poor guy barely had a free minute to himself, and after all day on his feet at the bakery, which was really a small factory with about twelve workers, all he wanted to do was rest. But to his credit, every now and then he'd bring us to a new stream, river, or swamp. He freely admitted he didn't have any outdoor skills to teach us, and at the time, that often bothered me. Other kids' dads might teach them how to deer hunt or instruct them on how to angle for trout or maybe even fly-fish, and I was jealous. Dad's skills—commitment, loyalty, and sheer physical endurance—were not readily apparent to me.

Looking back, I'm now thankful for those few times he did take us fishing, although sometimes we left the rods at home. Seriously. We did something I refer to as a "fish drive," somewhat akin to a deer drive, where a group of hunters walk through the woods pushing the game toward a waiting hunter. We did the same with fish. Mark and I would position ourselves in a stream with butterfly nets, and Dad would stand upstream about fifty feet. Then he would start walking toward us. His movements would scare the fish out of their hiding places, and they would head away from him and toward us.

The fish we were after was the mighty white sucker, universally scorned by all other anglers, but when you're twelve years old, any fish will do, and catching it is what counts. White suckers are not terribly attractive fish, with fleshy lips on the underside of their snout used to vacuum up food from the bottom of streams and lakes. What they lack in looks, they make up for in number and size, and the ones in our "sucker stream" were a foot long, which was Moby Dick–size to us.

Because this particular sucker stream was in a park, occasionally there would be onlookers who probably assumed, from our aggressive tactics, that we were dirt poor and needed these fish for our very survival. How could they know that stalking the great white sucker with a butterfly net was one of the most exciting things we had ever done?

The thrill of our sucker drives was often better than traditional fishing because Mark and I could see the fish coming toward us, and this visual aspect made it all the better. Sometimes the suckers had to race through shallow riffles, and the top of their backs would break the water. When they reached us, all hell would break loose as butterfly nets, arms, legs, and sometimes our whole bodies would flail the water.

The one problem with our sucker-driving procedures was that neither Mark nor I was the designated catcher, and we were too thickheaded to take turns. Since there were usually two or more fish shooting downstream, we figured there was enough to go around, but we often lunged at the same fish.

One spring day was especially memorable because several large suckers were in the brook just prior to spawning. Dad did his brook walk, like a sheepdog trying to herd a flock; when he scared a couple suckers into turning downstream, he hollered, "Get ready, they're coming!"

Mark and I went after the first fish we saw, and I was able to pin it against the bank with my net. I then grabbed it with my hand.

"Yeeooww! It bit me!" I wailed, letting go of the fish.

"Suckers don't bite," said Mark.

"Well this one did. See where my hand's red?"

"How can a sucker bite you when they have no teeth?"

He had a point there. "I don't know, but it did."

"Maybe he sucked you."

I don't think Mark was trying to be wise, but I took it that way and swung my butterfly net at the side of his head. He in turn jabbed me with his, and our little disagreement turned into butterfly net fencing.

My father was still walking the stream, and in the middle of my fight with Mark, a large sucker, a fifteen-incher, scooted over the shallows and came directly at me. All I had to do was lower my net and I had him. While I was scooping the sucker up, its weight and flopping motion caused the light fabric of the butterfly net to tear. The fish slid out the hole, but luckily it landed on a gravel bar, where Mark and I pounced on it. Victory was ours!

In the past we had let all of our suckers go, but I'd never caught one this big.

I shouted to my father, "We got a big one. Let's bring this home to show Mom."

"Then what will you do with it?" my father asked as he slogged up alongside us.

"We could eat it."

"I don't know if you can eat these things. I've never heard of anyone eating a sucker."

"Well then I'll keep it as a pet."

Dad had heard this line from me before. At one time or another, I had just about every creature known to inhabit New England as a pet. Chipmunks, snakes, robins, rabbits, voles, squirrels, snapping turtles, praying mantises; you name it, we had it. I'd keep it for a week, lose interest, then let it go.

We put the sucker in a bucket, brought it home, and I put it in my aquarium, where it terrorized my guppies. (At least it didn't eat anything. I had previously put a catfish and a small trout in with my guppies. The next morning the guppies were gone, the trout was half eaten, and the catfish seemed to be smiling beneath its whiskers.) After a week or two I let the sucker go in the closest brook to our house, Longmeadow Brook. This was the same brook in which Opie had caught the big rainbow trout, and Opie was none too happy. "Toug," he said, "suckers eat trout eggs. There won't be any more trout to catch." I'm not sure about suckers eating trout eggs, but we never caught another trout down at the Meadows again. In a sense this was an early lesson about the dangers of introducing a new species to a different location.

———

Fishing with my dad was never textbook angling; in fact, he rarely got to fish, since he was either the sucker herder or the designated rower. The first time we employed him as our human motor was also the first time we vacationed at the Rutledge Inn and Cottages on Lake Morey in Vermont.

The Green Mountain State took hold on us kids like no other place, and for the next ten years that's where our family took our one-week vacation. I'm sure my parents and my sister, Lynn, would have preferred trying a new setting from time to time, but we boys were convinced that a real vacation meant going to Lake Morey. It was the highlight of our year, and Vermont came to symbolize all good things.

While the Meadows helped forge a tie between Mark and me, Lake Morey was the place where I got to know my dad, at least a little bit. Fathers can be somewhat mysterious—difficult to read, difficult to grow close to. I'm convinced a large part of the reason for this gap between fathers and sons in the 1960s was that most women were stay-at-home housewives who did almost all the child rearing, while the father was the "breadwinner." It was a ridiculous division of labor, where my mom did everything around the house, including cooking, cleaning, washing, schlepping us kids around, shopping for us, etc. As a result, of the total time spent with one of my parents, the breakdown was something like 97 percent with my mom and 3 percent with my dad. It was almost as if we were raised by a single parent.

———

You don't get the full measure of a person, the full range of their personality, until you see them fresh, relaxed, and unhurried—a rare occurrence with my dad. At Lake Morey, however, work was the last thing on his mind, and it afforded me a glimpse into the window of his heart.

Our initial couple days fishing the lake were uneventful, catching only sunfish, so Dad drove us to the general store to ask advice from the old-timer who ran it.

"Can you help us pick out a lure or two?" asked my father. "The boys only seem to catch sunfish and perch."

The owner was sitting behind the counter. He looked up at Dad and then down at Mark and me. "Fishin' at Lake Morey?" he asked.

"Yup, these guys will fish for hours on end," explained Dad, gesturing to Mark and me.

The thought of us fishing endlessly, even though all we caught were panfish, seemed to impress the old man. A slight hint of a smile crossed his face. "I can remember doing the same thing at their age. Grew up right here and fished Lake Morey."

We thought he was going to bore us with a story, but he surprised us by saying, "So you want to catch a whopper bass?"

"Yes, sir," I answered. "We know where they are, we just can't catch 'em."

"How do you know where they are?"

"We dove down and saw them. About five or six big ones live by an underwater mine shaft," I answered excitedly.

Mark had seen them as well. "Some are this big"; he spread his arms to the two-foot range.

My father tried to explain. "I don't think it's an underwater cave, but there are some boards and boulders at the bottom of the lake near the inn."

Mark and I were convinced it was an abandoned gold or silver mine. What may have been nothing more than a large wooden box looked to us like the opening to a mine shaft. Whatever this underwater structure was, the bass loved it. With mask and snorkel, I'd made several visits to the site to watch the bass fin away the day. I wasn't the only person who knew the bass were there—a couple fishing lures, with frayed lines trailing, were embedded in the wooden planks. The bass somehow understood that a swimmer was no serious threat. Whenever I descended to the "depths of the mine" (about eight feet down) the bass let me approach to within a couple feet before they became annoyed and glided away. On one dive the largest bass of the group swam over and looked me in the eye, as if it might attack. With its mouth sloping downward, it had a mean look, as if to say, "Don't mess with me." That only made me more determined, so on my next dive I figured I'd show that fish who was boss. Cutting a sapling into a spear, I then took a rowboat out by the cave and dropped anchor. In the rowboat I had several rocks about the size of golf balls. I put these into the pockets of my bathing suit, donned my mask and gripped my spear, then carefully jumped over the side. The rocks did their work, and I quickly sank to the bottom. I jabbed at a bass and missed. Another bass was down by my feet, but I was afraid I'd spear myself. Almost out of breath, I started kicking toward the surface, but of course my ballast of rocks made it harder to rise. Frantically I jettisoned the weight, losing my bathing suit in the process. I swam up to the rowboat, gasping. Of course I couldn't climb into it bare ass; I had to wait a minute while I gathered my wits and then dived back down to get my bathing suit. I swear I saw the bass laughing at me. I decided not to tell Mark or anyone else about my stupidity for fear I'd be grounded or not allowed to take a rowboat out. This harebrained scheme was typical of me: I'd form a plan and put it into motion without thinking of the consequences. Having the rocks in my pocket was an easy mistake to solve, and I was never in any danger, but I wouldn't always be so lucky. The old adage "look before you leap" never quite sunk into my consciousness, and the idea of occasionally pausing before taking action never occurred to me. In later life, this would be both a blessing and a curse.

—⌣—

Seeing the largemouth bass was easy; catching them was something else entirely.

The old-timer at the general store walked Mark and me over to a shelf filled with little two- to five-inch boxes with clear plastic covers. Inside each box were minnow lures, some gold and others silver. He handed us a couple of boxes, each with a three-inch silver minnow inside.

"These will work," he said.

I, for one, believed him. The minnows looked lifelike, and the two sets of treble hooks meant business.

"Rapalas," said my father, reading the label on the lure box. "We'll give them a try."

—⌣—

My father was as good as his word. We set the alarm for five o'clock the next morning. The fact that my dad was willing to get up that early on his vacation seems nothing short of heroic to me now, considering this was his one week out of fifty-two to sleep late.

The Vermont air was cool, and everything was cloaked in gray shadows as the three of us quietly walked toward the lake. Even though it was summer, I had on a jacket to ward off the chill. The coat was either my spiffy tan Nehru jacket—an odd-looking coat full of buttons and without a collar—or a beige jean jacket. I know it was one of the two, because I must have worn those two coats exclusively from age eleven to thirteen. I was one of the few kids at that age who was not growing, and I was one of the smallest kids in my grade. It caused me considerable grief—much of it self-manufactured—but there was nothing I could do about it except continue to mark my height on the side of my bedroom door and pray that the line would one day be at least an inch higher.

Rounding out my fashion ensemble were skin-tight white jeans and black loafers. My shirt was untucked because that was the style in the 1960s, just as it is today. My bangs hung down across my eyebrows and into my eyes, imitating the newer British singers such as Peter Noone of Herman's Hermits. (I'd sing "Mrs. Brown You've Got a Lovely Daughter" in my best English accent until Mark almost puked. And when Mark couldn't take it anymore, I'd switch to "I'm Henry VIII, I Am," singing and flapping my arms like a chicken until he went running away clutching his head.)

Five of the inn's rowboats were lined up on the shore, and even in the heavy mist we all could tell which one was our favorite boat. The sound of the hull scraping on the sand as my father pushed the boat out seemed amplified in the predawn silence, and I hoped it wouldn't scare any fish away.

Mark and I sat in the stern facing the trail of swirling water behind the boat as Dad slowly pulled on the creaky oars. I turned around and looked at my father; he was smiling. Then I glanced at Mark, sitting patiently, watching the fog's strange patterns play over the water. That scene of my father and brother in the boat has become one of my few "mental snapshots"—a permanent picture of a moment in time. It serves as a place I can go back to in my mind and capture the essence of the two of them, as well as the wonder I felt on a new adventure.

Cutting through the fog was like opening a curtain into another world. Within seconds the shoreline disappeared and we might as well have been on the moon, engulfed by vapors, seeing only the dark, slick water flow past. I couldn't tell if it was us moving or the water itself; it seemed like we were anchored in a slow-flowing river. If we spoke at all, it was in whispers.

With our new Rapala Minnows trailing behind, the possibilities seemed endless. We didn't realize the rest of our tackle was ill-suited to bass fishing. Our poles were only about four feet long and made of plastic. I remember they were a sickly cream color. The reel was actually part of the rod itself, a one-piece contraption intended more for a bathtub than a lake. I always wondered what happened to those poles. Were they thrown out, or did some other kid get them at one of our tag sales? I wished we still had them. To me, those poles represented more of my youth than my first bike did.

We had Dad row us over the cave. Not once, but time and time again. After about the tenth pass, he suggested we try somewhere else, but we wouldn't hear of it. So back and forth we went, over and over this one spot. If anybody on shore could have seen through the fog, they might have thought my father was drunk, with the tiny rowboat going in circles.

The peacefulness of that gray morning allowed my father's mind to roam, and it wandered to his favorite subject: history. "You know," he said quietly, talking as much to himself as to us, "the first steamboat was invented right here. Everyone thinks that Robert Fulton invented it, but Samuel Morey, for whom the lake is named, was the first inventor. They say Morey was so mad when Fulton got the fame that he sunk his boat in this lake." Then Dad paused and added, "I saw it two days ago."

"What?" I asked, turning around to face him.

"Remember when I fell while water-skiing?"

How could I forget. It was his first time, and I was in the boat while Dad was being pulled. His skinny bowlegs were wobbling wildly and he was hunched over at the waist, but nevertheless he was skiing and hanging on for dear life. Then he tried to cross the wake and disappeared in a violent spray. When he wiped out, his skis shot into the air, but he didn't come up. I thought my dad had died right in front of me. The boat started to curl back to where he fell, while I held my breath. Dad was holding his breath too, still clutching onto the ski rope while being dragged through the depths of the lake!

The driver finally realized the drag on the ski rope was my father, and he cut the motor. Dad finally surfaced, weeds draped around his neck, gasping and clutching his shoulder. The driver eased the boat back to him and shouted to ask if he was alright. Dad coughed a couple times, spit up some water, and said, "No one told me to let go of the rope if I fall."

That night, despite his aching shoulder, which still pained him, Dad made fun of his stupidity. "This dumb Greek got a tour of the bottom of the lake!" he joked to fellow guests, telling the story.

But now sitting in the rowboat, looking at him smile then wince as he pulled the oars, I realized he had a new story angle for his near disaster.

"That's right," he said. "When I was being dragged all over the bottom of the lake, I went right by a boat with a big side paddle wheel. Must have been Morey's. I didn't have time to see if the old fellow was still at the wheel."

For a second Mark and I thought he was serious, but then Dad chuckled softly.

"Maybe," whispered Dad, "it's underneath us right now, just waiting to be discovered."

We talked about Morey, the steamboat, and whether anything would be left of the boat after so many years. I felt a rare closeness between us and thought if we lived on this lake, the feeling would always be there. I asked Dad if he ever thought about moving to Vermont, but all he said was "I'll never move."

I looked out at the fog. I knew somewhere beyond the whiteness were the smooth curves of the mountains that encircled the lake, and I envisioned a cabin far up the slopes. From that lofty perch I could look down and see the lake and think of all the good times.

"Ever think about buying a little cabin up here?" I asked.

My father kept rowing then said, "Costs money, money we don't have."

He was right about the money, but even if we had it, he would never make such an investment. You see, my father resisted change. He was set in his ways and had no inclination to alter set routines. I never completely understood why. It exasperated his brothers, who ran the bakery with him, and I can remember once when I was at the bakery, my uncles were trying to convince my dad to try a new method of baking or a new piece of equipment. He would usually say something like "It will just cause more headaches." They would respond, "How do you know until we try?" Then the conversation would degenerate into an argument, until my father would just go mute and return to work. I can even recall friends of his telling me,

"Your dad sure is stubborn." This aspect of his personality was ingrained, and I suspect it might have had something to do with his own father, Elias, from the "old country," whom my dad greatly admired. I think my dad wanted to live his life in a similar way and to follow his examples, and of course that meant few changes. But there was a positive side to his obstinacy. A few years later, when my family faced tragedy, the stubbornness of my father enabled him to persevere when others would have long given up.

Instinctively I knew that getting him to buy a cabin was going to be next to impossible. The man was still using the same bread mixer his father did; he wasn't about to buy a new vacation home when he only had one week off a year.

Part of my yearning for a cabin, however flawed, was my effort to try and capture and maybe repeat these moments of us fishing. I figured that times like right now—floating through the morning mist and listening to creaky oars in the stillness—could be duplicated over and over if we just had a special place to go. The cabin concept, I later realized, was my pursuit of happiness, my quest for simple pleasures, and a desire to replicate these fleeting feelings of camaraderie I felt with my brother and father when we were outdoors. I thought the setting was the key to these possibilities rather than my outlook or mindset, and who's to say I was wrong?

—◦—

The conversation in our boat eased off. Dad continued rowing as if he were a machine, and the only sound was dripping water and the squeaks of the oars. Mark was still watching the mist—eyeing it with the creativeness of an artist, which would someday be his chosen profession.

The slow, rhythmic motions of the boat had a hypnotic effect on me. I forgot all about my father and brother. My thoughts and eyes were twenty feet behind the boat, where my trailing line entered the dark water. I knew the Rapala was somewhere back there, pulsating and surging forward with each pull of the oars. I imagined I was a bass, gliding right behind the lure, weaving my way through the top of the weed line.

Maybe the lure needed more action. I pumped the rod. This, I figured, would make the lure dart forward then briefly flutter down.

Then the lure stopped, jolting me out of my reverie.

"Wait," I said as my line stretched.

Dad pushed the oars backward, bringing the boat to a sudden halt.

"What is it?" asked my father, his voice hopeful.

I knew the lure was fouled in the weeds by the way it just stopped dead. There was no movement on the line, no throb or pull. My twitching of the lure had probably allowed it to fall just deep enough to hit the top of the weed bed.

"I'm snagged," I answered dully, the magic gone. In the cold morning stillness, even these words sounded profound and important. I've noticed that the more time you spend on the water or in the woods, fewer words are spoken, and when you do talk, people listen. I could feel my brother relax beside me. The words "I'm snagged" deflated our hope and anticipation—I sensed that my father was about done in from pulling us back and forth over the cave.

Dad slowly rowed in reverse, and I reeled in slack line until we were above the snag. The lure would not come free, so my father took the line and started pulling it up hand over hand.

Then the water exploded. We had all been craning our necks over the side of the boat and were shocked to see a great fish rocket out of the water amid a tangle of weeds.

"Fish!"

"Net!"

"Bass!"

Our voices boomed. My father, who had yelled the loudest, recovered and told us not to shout. But by that time I'm sure we had woken up all those guests who were in cottages near the shore.

Dad was so shocked by the fish's appearance that he dropped the line and was now pulling it in again.

The fish was still on, though. We could see it racing around just below the water's surface. I had hollered "net," but of course we had none, so it was up to my father to haul it in. Dad must have sensed that if he brought the bass up now, it would jump again, maybe breaking free. So he let the fish race around beneath the boat, tiring itself as it pulled the tangle of weeds through the water. Then he slowly eased the fish up and, using both hands, lifted it into the boat, where it lay at my feet.

We rowed into shore, whispering like bandits just after a heist. Running straight to our cabin, we woke my mother up for a picture-taking session.

I still have that old black-and-white photo. In it, I'm grinning ear to ear with a wild look in my eye, as if I'm going to burst with excitement.

The photo reveals more than joy. It reveals that I wasn't the outdoorsman I thought I was, but instead relied on my father to grip that old bass. Only his arm is in the picture, but it's clear he's holding the fish and my hands are wrapped around it just for show.

That photo got me thinking. It was my father who rowed the boat, pulled up the fish, and held it up for my picture. I really didn't do much, but at the time I never even considered my dad's role—those thoughts didn't come until many years later.

CHAPTER EIGHT

AFTER THAT TRIP TO VERMONT MY CABIN VISION BECAME SIGNIFI-
cantly stronger, prompting me to cut out pictures of rustic log cabins and
post them on my bedroom bulletin board. This was also the time that my
pleasure reading began to focus on anything to do with life in the mountains. Books about the Lewis and Clark Expedition or early mountain
men were just some of the tales that fueled an active imagination. And at
the time, an active imagination was about my only attribute. In a country
obsessed with athletic prowess, I had little. Baseball was popular in our
town, and I had no aptitude for it. Even playing against younger kids, I
rarely got a hit. In fact, when a pitcher put some heat on the ball, I was
secretly hoping for a walk so I didn't have to get too close to the pitch.
But I put on a good act, and would throw my bat down when the umpire
invariably called me out on strikes.

This veneer of machismo would get me in trouble in school and in
the outdoors, particularly on our family's next trip to Lake Morey the
following year, when I was thirteen or fourteen years old, champing at
the bit to assert my independence. I still fished with Dad and Mark, but
I wanted my own adventures, stories I could casually tell to the friends
back home that would make them jealous. I was headstrong to a fault, but
"The Great Voyage" would temper these traits.

It all started with a cardboard napkin ring.

At the Rutledge Inn, all three daily meals were included in the
lodging price. Each family, couple, or single guest sat at the same table
in the dining room for the duration of their stay, usually a week or two.
Individual guests would sign their name on a cardboard ring, and that
ring would be wrapped around a clean cloth napkin placed at the same
seat for each meal.

The year of The Great Voyage, I insisted on signing my own name
rather than letting my mother do the honors for all of us. That was my
first mistake.

There was another family staying at the inn the same week who
were old friends of ours. The father of the family had begun calling me a

nickname the previous year that sounded rather pleasing. I didn't know that he gave the nickname tongue-in-cheek because I had the habit of always announcing some grandiose plan. He got a chuckle out of calling me "Mike the Great."

It sounded good, so I put that on my napkin ring: "Mike the Great." I'm sure the kitchen staff and waitresses had a good laugh over that one.

As far back as I can remember, I was writing lists of things I wanted to accomplish. They say that's good strategy for ambitious, goal-oriented achievers, but I hadn't even reached puberty. This year's vacation accomplishment would have to be loftier than ever; after all, I had a new nickname to live up to.

I didn't know who Peter the Great was, but I assumed he had done something no other man had ever done. And so I must do the same. I decided to canoe around the lake. Alone. Surely no one had done that before—the lake was at least a mile long. It was the biggest lake I had ever canoed on; now that I think about it, it was the only lake I had ever canoed on.

I secretly expected my mother to put a quick end to my plan; then I could spend the rest of the week complaining to anyone that would listen about how I *would* have circled the lake but my mother had killed the plan. That way I could still talk about The Great Voyage without ever lifting a paddle.

But she talked it over with my father, got me to commit to keeping the canoe close to the shoreline, and then gave me her blessing. Even predictable parents can throw you a curve.

When I told Mark of my plans, he offered to come along—not so much because he wanted to but out of a sense of obligation.

"That's an awful long way to paddle alone," he said, shaking his head like I was crazy. "If I go with you, we can take turns fishing while the other person paddles."

I thought of our trips to the Meadows. It would be good to have him along, and I did have a trace of foreboding about the trip. We were a good team—even if I never acknowledged it. But this was different. This was Vermont. This was on "The List." And I had already told my father I was going alone. It certainly wouldn't look good if, after getting his approval for the solo voyage, I suddenly added a passenger.

Word got around of what I was going to do, and people gathered at the dock for my scheduled departure the next morning. They watched as I packed the canoe with supplies: a jug of water and a knife. The water made sense, but I can't for the life of me remember why I brought the knife. Perhaps I thought the lake had its own Loch Ness Monster, which might try to grab me. I do know that at that age, I had not totally ruled out monsters. And it didn't help that I still remembered my camp counselor describing how six-foot frogs lived at the bottom of some lakes and were known to ram small boats, spill the occupant out, and then swallow them whole. He had described the scenario so convincingly, I thought maybe, just maybe, it was possible.

Half the guests at the inn had noticed the commotion at the dock, and most strolled down to give me last-minute advice and wish me well. Just as I was about to push off, my mother embarrassed me by saying, "Put that life vest on or you're not going anywhere."

It was one of those bulky, bright orange life vests that make you feel like you have a broken neck. This was not the way I wanted to begin, but I put it around my neck and struggled to fasten the straps.

As I pushed the aluminum canoe away from the dock, a couple people cheered. I paddled for everything I was worth to show them the good speed I could make. Then a booming voice rose from the group and carried over the water, "THERE GOES MIKE THE GREAT!"

At that moment I started growing tired of the name and wished he hadn't said it.

I continued paddling hard, and it wasn't long before I looked back; the dock was just a speck on the horizon. I immediately took my life vest off. Did Magellan or Columbus wear a life vest? Certainly not. And if they did, the vests were probably more stylish than this fluorescent orange neck brace that impeded my paddling.

Ah, this is the life, I said to myself. I felt free, strong, and quite grown-up. Out on my own, just nature and me. The lake never appeared so blue, nor the surrounding mountains so green. I would have to remember to tell the poor landlubbers just how wonderful the lake looks from this far out.

I enjoyed the rhythm of the paddling as I occupied myself by closely inspecting the cottages I passed. Over the winter I had hounded my father and mother about buying a cabin or cottage in Vermont. I knew it was likely a waste of time trying to convince my father, but I figured maybe my mother would come around, as she seemed to have the final say on big purchases. When their response was less than enthusiastic, I began to read the real estate section of the Sunday paper, cut out property listed in Vermont, and leave the listings on my mother's dresser. After a week of this, she finally pointed out that with just a one- or two-week vacation, it was hardly worth having a summer home.

But now, as I cruised by the cottages, I thought I might be able to convince them of the wisdom of my plan if they could see these places from a water view. I would appeal to my father's sense of relaxation, telling him there was really no grass to cut at these shorefront cottages, and wouldn't it be great to have his beer out on a deck overlooking the water? Each bungalow seemed to look better than the next, and I couldn't wait to get him out here. And I'd tell my mother how we could catch our own meals and have fresh fish for dinner. (I did not consider that it would be her doing the cooking, since I'd already seen my lack of culinary skill with the bullhead Mark and I roasted at the Meadows.) She could come up here and not have to drive us boys around, because everything we needed would be right in front of the cottage: the lake. And I'd make a point to mention these benefits to my parents when my older sister, Lynn, was not around, because I knew she'd hate being taken away from her friends.

The canoe cut through the water quite nicely as my long powerful strokes—aided by a slight breeze—propelled it northward. Whenever I passed another vessel, I would act the proper seaman and wave or tip my cap. I wondered if the other boaters knew that I was going to circle the lake.

There were a couple little coves along the western shoreline that looked inviting, but my arms were beginning to tire, so I stayed on a straight course. About halfway up the lake I was pretty pooped, so I decided to drift awhile and refresh myself from the water jug. It occurred to me that I might miss lunch back at the inn. Today was BLT day, with chocolate pudding for desert. I was hungry and wished I had packed a sandwich. The trip was taking a little longer than I had thought.

After ten minutes I resumed paddling and occupied my thoughts by examining the shore where a large home perched on a hill near a sprawling children's summer camp. I made a few mental notes of interesting sites—perhaps someone back at the inn would want to hear what this side of the lake looked like.

Occasionally a powerboat would roar by pulling a water-skier. The wake from the boats rocked my canoe, making it bob like a duck. Small sailboats sliced past me as the wind picked up. The sun was now hiding behind a large bank of clouds, and the air lost its July warmth.

The back end of the lake narrowed where a point of land jutted out into the water. Technically the end of the lake was still about a quarter of a mile ahead. But with the wind increasing and the air getting downright chilly, I decided that *seeing* the end of the lake meant I had been there. The plan called for me to make a clockwise circle of the long, skinny lake, and it was time to head to the opposite shore and begin the trip back.

Swinging my canoe to the right, I felt the full force of the wind for the first time. I managed to keep the canoe straight by paddling only on the left, as the wind was coming up the lake from my right. For the first time I also noticed how high the front of the canoe rode, cursing myself for not putting a rock in the bow as I had read in one of my outdoor books. Better yet, I wished Mark was in the bow paddling.

My arms felt like lead, but when I reached the opposite shore I dared not stop paddling because the sky had darkened and seven-inch waves kicked up. Turning the canoe into the wind proved to be next to impossible, and the first attempt ended with me being blown about, facing the wrong direction. I decided it was best to rest my arms before the next try, but in the meantime I was being pushed back toward the north.

My concern over the situation bordered on panic. The waves, which had grown to colossal ten-inchers, occasionally had tiny whitecaps. I picked the bright orange life vest up from the bottom of the canoe and fastened it around my neck. The fabric was dripping wet, and it felt cold and clammy. But my real worry, the one I kept trying not to think about, was that this aluminum canoe was going to flip. Why hadn't I taken a rowboat?

I had to get the canoe turned or I'd be blown even farther back, perhaps into the rocky shore. With a rush of adrenaline born of real fear, I paddled for all I was worth and succeeded in turning the vessel.

The bow had to be pointed perfectly into the wind or a gust would catch it and blow it sideways. Ten minutes of paddling and I had traveled no more than fifty feet. My arms were numb, screaming for rest.

The canoe was being buffeted about, and I was certain it was going to capsize with the next big gust. Not only was I afraid for my personal safety, I was concerned about the canoe. How could I ever tell the inn owners that their canoe was at the bottom of the lake? And then I thought of having to face all those guests.

Tears were in my eyes. I was beaten. I let the wind carry me into the shoreline, where gusts pushed the canoe up against an overhanging tree. Waves rammed the hull against submerged boulders, causing a sickening scraping sound. The shore was too steep to slide the canoe up, so I got out and just stood there in a foot of water, gripping the gunnels, on the verge of sobbing. I was glad my father wasn't around to see such weakness.

If I could somehow find a level spot to drag the canoe out, I thought I might be able to walk back to the inn via the shore road. But I was so tired, I simply sat down on a rock. The canoe slammed against the tree while rubbing on the rocks below with each new wave.

It was bad enough being stranded, but now it looked as though the canoe would be damaged. I thought how stupid I was for not packing some rope. No, I had to take a knife and forget the rope. Any outdoorsman worth his salt knows that a rope and matches should be packed with the knife. None of what I learned in *Dogsled Danger* had done me any good.

Salvation came in the form of a powerboat. An older man was behind the wheel. "I saw you struggling from my cottage window. Where are you trying to go?" he shouted through the wind, slowly steering the boat to within thirty feet of me.

Relief spread through my body, and I gave a nervous smile. "I was trying to get back to the Rutledge Inn."

"OK, I think I can help. I'll tow you back."

My spirits soared; I was not going to have to abandon ship.

He threw me the ski rope, and I tied it to the crossbar in the bow of the canoe. I sat back down in the stern, and, ever so slowly, he started moving out.

It must have taken twenty minutes to tow me back, but I wasn't complaining. As we came within sight of the Rutledge Inn shoreline, it seemed like the wind died down. Or maybe it was never quite the storm I thought it was. It felt like I'd been gone for days, although only a couple hours had passed.

When the few folks on shore realized there was a canoe being towed behind the boat, they came down to the dock for a better look. The man in the powerboat cut the engine, and I untied the rope. He then simply waved, gunned the motor, and was gone. I never told him thanks, never told him how I thought I might die out there—but I'm certain he knew.

And so I paddled the last fifty feet to shore. There were about ten people on the dock, but there might as well have been a hundred—word would get around that the young explorer in the orange life vest had been towed back to shore. Still, I was happy. I was so relieved to be back safely, I even managed a sheepish wave.

The group waved back.

Then someone in the back bellowed, "Looks like Mike the Great had a tough voyage!"

That night at dinner I put my napkin ring in my pocket, and later I threw it in the woods.

~~~

About fifty years after The Great Voyage, I had a conversation with Gary Guilmette, who was on the dock when I got towed in. I told him the full story, including how terrified I had been. Later in an e-mail he wrote: "I remember we kept looking down the lake for you and how worried your mother was. But my lasting memory of that day is you coming back, riding on the crest of the wake behind the guy's motor-boat. The canoe was high on the wake, and you were sitting back there with the usual ear-to-ear grin. If you ever worried about anything, you were very good at not showing it."

Gary's insight was spot on. I was a good actor. And that acting ability would get me in jams a lot worse than the one on Lake Morey.

CHAPTER NINE

THE LESSON OF THE FAILED CANOE VOYAGE WAS SHORT-LIVED. RATHER than truly learning lasting humility, my long-term takeaway was never to canoe in the wind and to hold all pronouncements until after they'd been accomplished.

Now, as a teenager, I thought having a veneer of machismo was a good survival technique in the ever-increasing peer pressure at school. And the global situation in 1969 didn't help with any stability. Weird stuff was going on. Woodstock, a weekend concert with some of the best bands of the era—described by newspapers as "a coming together for rock, drugs, sex, and peace"—certainly caught my attention. In fact I longed to be there because I could think of nothing more fun than rolling around in the mud with some naked girls. And the music must have been phenomenal, with Jimmy Hendrix, The Band, and Jefferson Airplane all jamming away to the stoned-out crowd. I imagined myself there, listening to Grace Slick live while in the mud with a beautiful naked woman, smoking a doobie the size of Rhode Island with a peace symbol painted on my face. What could be better? Lots of things, but when you are fourteen years old, that sounds pretty cool. (I had just smoked my first joint with Cogs, and I swear I saw his legs grow by a foot.)

My dad watched the news with Walter Cronkite every night, and I sometimes joined him. To say that 1969 was a disaster of a year for our country is an understatement. The news had a trickle-down effect on me, enforcing my belief to live for the moment because tomorrow may not come. Here are just some of the headlines from that year: Members of Charles Manson's cult murdered actress Sharon Tate and others, leaving the words "Helter Skelter" spelled out on her refrigerator and "Rise" and "Death to Pigs" written in blood on the walls of her home. One of the Black Panther leaders was killed in a wild shoot-out in Chicago. Ohio's Cuyahoga River went up in flames. Hundreds of Vietnamese civilians were slaughtered by rogue US Army troops in what became known as the My Lai Massacre. Nixon began "Vietnamization" to "end the war with honor," while massive antiwar rallies were held across the country. Vice

President Agnew, throwing fuel on the fire, called anyone who demonstrated against the war "ideological eunuchs" and said any journalists writing antiwar op-eds were pedaling "seditious drivel." It seemed the country was being split in two, between those who supported and those who opposed the war, while Nixon and Agnew drove the divide even deeper. (If you think today's news cycle is the worst ever, 1969 was likely just as depressing.) Adults lost their sense of trust in the government, and younger people lost trust of anyone in authority. Things sure were changing, and fast.

No wonder I was adrift. But there was good news that year too, and it unfolded during my family's vacation to Vermont, further cementing my association of the Green Mountain State with more-pleasant happenings. The six of us watched Neil Armstrong bound across the moon's surface on a grainy black-and-white TV in the sitting area of the Rutledge Inn on Lake Morey. The room was jammed with guests, and you could have heard a pin drop as Cronkite described the descent of the lunar module and then cheers when Armstrong descended the ladder and did his kangaroo hop on that barren landscape.

While most people were in awe, I remember thinking what a terrible place the moon is. There is not a blade of grass, tree, bird, or fish. Why in the world do we want to even be there?

Another matter was also on my mind. Guilt. Mark had just won the contest to guess how many beans were in a giant glass jar. There were 821 beans in the jar, and Mark guessed 820. But the truth of the matter is that the word "guess" is a stretch. You see, dear reader, Mark and I had snuck into the attic of the inn two days earlier and discovered said jar. I unscrewed the top and found a piece of paper on top of the beans with the number 821 on it.

The next day the jar appeared in the lobby, and guests were encouraged to write down their estimate of the number of beans in the jar and win ten dollars. Now you might wonder why Mark was the winner and not me. Well, I had the feeling that if I won, people would be suspicious, but if Mark won, no one would be the wiser. And so I pressured him to fill out an entry based on our ill-gotten knowledge. Just to make sure we covered our tracks, I told him to guess one digit off the real number. I should have made it ten or twenty, because Mark's "guess" was a little too close for comfort, with people coming up to him and saying, "It's incredible how close your guess was. It's like you got inside the jar and counted every bean but one!"

We were frauds filled with remorse, but I could see no graceful way out of it and kept my lips firmly sealed. I knew my father, if he found out, would disown me. Honesty was paramount in his view of a person's character. In his mind, cheating would be even worse than the year I broke my school's detention record.

I was the mastermind behind the bean-counting caper, but Mark felt the self-reproach even more because people kept congratulating him. He seemed ready to crack and, dare I say it . . . spill the beans, but I hissed, "Nobody is ever going to know about this." And nobody ever did. Until now.

~

The Rutledge Inn was idyllic in every sense of the word, and the antidote to the bizarre happenings worldwide in 1969. For one week we were able to throw back the calendar and be in a more innocent time. The TV that we watched the moon landing on was put away because the inn had a policy of no television, which was wonderful. When the sun went down we simply talked with other guests of all ages. In fact, older folks loved the inn for that very reason—they could sit on the inn's front porch in a rocker and talk to kids. And those old folks were characters who loved a good joke and truly were interested in what we were up to. They wanted to hear about the fish we caught as much as we wanted an audience. The interaction was heartwarming, and today's impersonal social media can't hold a candle to it, because it robs children of the interaction of listening, storytelling, and good-natured teasing. On social media kids have almost no contact with the elderly, but at the inn I loved those old codgers on the porch. One guy named Harry would bark like a dog whenever I went by. And I remember he once called me over and asked if I had seen the scar on the hill on the opposite side of the lake. (It was hard to miss that blight on the landscape, because it was Interstate 91 being extended into northern Vermont.) When I said that I had, Harry said, "Well, Sonny, that's progress." I wasn't sure if he was being sarcastic, but from that point onward, I hated the word "progress."

Although there were some rooms above the inn, most people rented a cottage for a week, and each cottage had a name like Sunny Slope or Sweet William. There were about twenty-two or twenty-three cottages, and most either surrounded an open field where games were played or were on the waterfront. One year we stayed in a cottage that was the farthest from the inn and nestled in the woods next to the lake. My family wasn't wild about the isolation of the cottage compared to those near the inn, but I liked the feel of it, as it seemed more like the cabins the mountain men I'd been reading about built. Either way, I knew Vermont would be the place I'd find my own cabin someday.

At Lake Morey I experimented with my writing and kept a vacation diary. I recently unearthed it, and here are some entries:

Dad rowed the boat while we fished. But bats or swallows attacked us and he rowed to shore. He was afraid they would hit his nose.

Today Mark was sick and barfed all night. I feel fine.

Tried to fish in the Connecticket River but instead we looked at gravestones with Daddy.

Bob (four years old) was so excited to come here he wet his pants.

And in those diaries it's clear I was obsessed with the older girls who worked there:

Went canoe bobbing with Lisa, our waitress. Did not tell her we won the bean counting.

The hostess said she would send me a picture of her in a bathing suit. She is going to U of Maine. Look her up if I ever go there.

Valerie, a girl who works here, who I do not spark to, talked to me.

Lake Morey will forever hold a special place in my heart, with all those happy days of swimming, canoeing, and fishing. On one trip I was already dressed in my bathing suit, and before the car rolled to a stop, I bolted out and charged down to the lake, throwing myself in as if reuniting with a long-lost lover. That place was special. (But don't try looking for it. The inn is gone, the cottages torn down or sold off. A McMansion occupies the prime site where the beach area was. Apparently, families' vacation tastes changed along with the value of waterfront property . . . progress.)

I remember one trip not for the adventure of conquering fish, canoe bobbing with a waitress, or attempting to paddle the lake, but rather for its gentleness and my connection to both nature and my brother Mark. He had borrowed or bought himself a deer call and taken it into the woods alone. He came back with a wild story that he was able to call in several deer to within twenty feet of where he sat. Of course I didn't believe him and said, "Prove it." He surprised me by responding that he'd be happy to.

Now, seeing a deer was a big deal for us flatlanders from Massachusetts in the 1960s. There were far fewer deer in southern New England than there are today, and the few deer we had seen were usually dead, tied to the roof rack of someone returning from a hunt in northern New England. So the chance to see one up close was a rare opportunity for me.

The next day Mark and I began hiking toward the same spot in the woods that he had labeled "the magical forest." It wasn't far from the inn, but because I was focused so intently on the lake, I'd never even climbed up and over the ridge and seen this patch of woods. It had mature maples and beeches with little undergrowth and made me feel small, not unlike the mood we experienced during our rambles beneath the cottonwoods by the Connecticut River in the Meadows. The canopy of leaves above us was so thick, only an occasional patch of fern-covered ground was dappled by sunlight.

Mark was leading the way. This in itself was something new, and I had to hold myself back from not charging ahead. He walked as if in slow motion, paying attention to every footfall. I did the same and couldn't help but enjoy the chance to become fully aware of my surroundings and be in the moment rather than planning my next accomplishment, goal, or conquest. Instead I was cognizant of the forest smell of ferns and decaying leaves, of noting the different hues of green foliage, the lack of wind, and how soft the ground was beneath my feet. I loved the feeling, however fleeting.

We sat at the base of a huge beech tree, its smooth gray bark looking like the leg of an elephant. There were few trees directly in front of us, and visibility was excellent. Mark whispered to me to stay still and not talk. We sat there a good ten minutes, letting ourselves get acclimated to the silence of the forest. It felt good to be detached from the rest of the world, and the stillness and apparent emptiness of the glade added to the otherworldly atmosphere. Mark softly blew on the deer call. The sound that came out—not too different from a lamb bleating—was supposed to mimic a fawn in distress. The announcement floated through the woods and drifted up the hillside. A chill went up my spine in anticipation of a deer running to our little glade to check us out. Mark made one more call then put the deer call in his pocket, making himself comfortable. He had read the directions carefully and didn't want to make the mistake of overdoing it but rather pique the deer's natural curiosity.

Several minutes went by; I grew antsy and nudged him, opening my hands as if to say, "Well, where are they?"

Mark stayed perfectly still, and I wondered if he was falling asleep. Then he put his hand out, motioning for me to calm down, something I was never good at—and am still working on. I gave Mark the benefit of the doubt and closed my eyes, trying to soak up the peacefulness of his magical forest. When I opened my eyes a couple minutes later, a doe and a fawn stood in the little glade we were in. Then another doe materialized, ghostlike, from over the crest of the ridge. All of them stared at us. The does must have seen humans before, but they didn't act like it. Rather they seemed inquisitive. Perhaps they were trying to reconcile the sound of a bleating fawn with the two unmoving creatures under the beech tree. The does took a couple tentative steps toward us, and the fawn followed.

I assumed they were does, but perhaps one was a buck. After all, it was summer; bucks shed their antlers in the winter, and at the time I wasn't sure when they started growing back. No matter; they were magnificent, with thick necks and tawny coats.

My eyes were as big as the deer's. Here was a kind of contact with nature that fishing didn't provide. In this little glade in the woods, I felt like I was just one more creature on the planet, not *the* creature the world revolved around. By sitting still, it seemed I had entered their world, their consciousness.

One doe, larger than the other, took another two delicate steps toward us, its massive ears twitching. Such a handsome creature, so graceful.

Mark slowly turned his head and jutted his chin out toward the ridgeline. There was a third doe staring at us, with only its head showing above a log at the top of the ridge. I didn't move a muscle, and this deer silently moved a few feet closer.

It was an incredible experience. I'd seen deer before, but they were always running away; now they were carefully moving toward us. They were obviously perplexed, and with each tentative step they were trying to unlock the mystery of the fawn call and the two unmoving creatures under the beech tree. One of the does snorted and pawed the ground once or twice, but neither Mark nor I moved. That seemed only to increase the deer's interest, and it moved closer still, forgetting its natural wariness in an attempt to understand what was happening. Maybe it was frustrated and agitated, getting downright pissed off trying to figure out the source of the fawn noises.

Two of the does were only about twenty feet away, with the fawn hanging farther back. I was beginning to feel like the hunted rather than the hunter, and wondered if deer ever attacked humans. But that twinge of anxiety was nothing compared to the astonishment and wonder of having wild creatures as large as me in close proximity. The experience made me see each deer as an individual, and I contemplated whether they had some unseen way of communicating and if one of the three was the leader.

Then I ruined the moment. My camera was hanging around my neck, and the temptation to get this point-blank picture was too much. As soon as I moved my arm toward the camera, the deer wheeled away, making incredible seven-foot bounds back into the maple forest. I clicked the shutter, hoping to at least get their white flag tails on film.

I was afraid Mark would be angry with me, but he was smiling.

"Wow" was all I could say. I felt a newfound albeit grudging admiration for Mark. He showed me what patience could do, what stillness could accomplish. He demonstrated that you can let things come to you rather than my method of going right at the thing I was after.

I lost the photo I took that day, but I still have the mental picture of two boys sitting quietly in a forest with no adult telling us the right or wrong way to enjoy wild creatures.

CHAPTER TEN

AT AGE FOURTEEN I FIGURED I WAS TOUGH ENOUGH TO WORK AN OCCA-sional day at the Tougias Baking Company, run by my father and his three brothers. I was dead wrong. In 1969 and 1970 there was little automation in the bakery, and the physical labor was brutal as employees hustled from station to station at an intense pace set by my father. Lifting, bending, squatting, pushing, pulling. Baking mass quantities of bread and rolls was like boot camp, and it kicked my butt and gave me new insight into my dad.

Uncles Pons, Angelo, and Pete delivered the bread to restaurants and supermarkets, secured new customers, and managed the administrative side of the business, while my father was responsible for about ten employees who helped him make the product. The bakery is one of the oldest continually family-run businesses in the United States. It was started by my grandfather Elias, who immigrated to America from Greece in 1902, unable to speak a word of English. He started baking French and Italian bread in 1904, delivering individual loaves to homes by horse and wagon.

With the money Elias earned, he was able to return to Greece and bring my grandmother Artemis back to the United States. His business and his growing family flourished until the Great Depression. My father explained to me that Elias continued to bake and give bread to people, even though he knew it was unlikely they could pay him. Eventually the bank foreclosed on both the bakery and the house he had bought. Elias watched from the street as his property was auctioned off.

Rather than throw in the towel, he rented a place on Hancock Street in Springfield, Massachusetts, that had an old brick oven and started making bread again.

The 1940s were just as difficult as the 1930s for Elias. In 1941 his oldest son, George, died, and the next year he lost his wife. Meanwhile three of his other sons all served in the army during World War II. My father was the only son still at home, in high school, helping out Elias when he could. The bakery was in danger of failing again due to wartime rationing of gas and difficulty attaining the ingredients for bread, such as sugar, flour, and lard, and coal for the oven.

I recently found a three-page letter my dad wrote to my son about the bakery; in it he explained that after the war, all four of Elias's remaining sons joined the business, found a permanent location, and together made it prosper. (My cousins run the business today.) Dad ended his letter by writing how his father kept the bakery moving forward by saying, "Not bad for someone who came from the old country." That line was in keeping with the way Dad always talked about Elias, with pure respect and admiration.

When I look back at those days of working with my dad, I realize the drive to the bakery with my father at the ungodly hour of 4:00 a.m. was as important as working by his side. It was the only time I can remember that we spent time alone. He knew I was into wildlife, and we'd discuss what he'd seen over the years in the illumination of his headlights, such as foxes, rabbits, raccoons, and even a low-flying owl. Dad talked about where the cop cars would usually be hidden, and he varied his speed accordingly. Instead of driving direct to the bakery, we often made stops in Springfield to pick up an employee or two whose driver's license was suspended or who did not own cars. In downtown Springfield we'd see ladies of the night still plying their trade. I asked Dad if the hookers really had any customers at 4:00 a.m., and he said something like "They wouldn't be out here in the freezing cold if they didn't." Then he'd admonish me to stay away from this area once I got my driver's license, explaining that there were men who would think nothing of stabbing you for just looking at them the wrong way.

Sometimes we would pick up Albert, a former Canadian who spoke a mix of French and broken English and seemed ancient to me but was probably only sixty-five years old. God, he was a character. Standing no more than five feet tall, with a wrinkled flat face and dyed jet-black hair, he would say the same thing to me every morning: "Michael, apple?" while thrusting an apple into my hand. I loved going into his apartment because he would always have something to show me, most memorably his dog, which would whisper to him. Of course I said, "Show me," so he said to the dog, "Tell me a secret." The dog hopped up on the kitchen table and, sure enough, put his snout against Albert's ear and started to make what

I would describe as a low-pitched murmuring sound. The dog really was whispering something to Albert, and Albert explained that it was the weather report. Later my dad explained that Albert had put a piece of candy in his ear, and the dog was murmuring in ecstasy as he licked it.

Often Albert's wife, "Mama," would be awake when we picked him up. The two of them might be bickering one day and loving the next, but she always sent him to the bakery with a bag containing his lunch, along with candy and apples for his fellow workers. Dad told me that Mama often called him, pleading for him to drag Albert out of some bar where he had spent the evening. "She had me get him out of the Starlight Lounge one night, and I brought him back to Mama," explained my father. "An hour later she called again and said he was back at the Starlight and I needed to haul him home before something terrible happened. And so I did. When she called a third time, I said no, that I needed to get at least one hour's sleep before work."

So Dad was Albert's part-time caretaker. No wonder he rarely had time to talk with me.

Other times we'd stop and get Conrad, another character who fascinated me. Dad often explained that Conrad might have just gotten home from a night on the town but could still outwork most of the other guys at the bakery. I always enjoyed talking with Conrad, who tried to impart some street smarts into me. Conrad thought the world of my father, and I remember asking my dad about their friendship because they were so different—family man versus bachelor who lived for the moment. Dad explained that Conrad was as tough as nails, and he was loyal. He related a story of how he had bailed Conrad out of jail a couple times, and that in one instance the police told my father that Conrad beat up another guy and then tried to do the same to the four cops who arrested him. The cops finally got Conrad in the paddy wagon by using their nightsticks on his head, but he was back at work three days later!

On those early-morning rides to the bakery, my father often talked about his father, and he always stressed to me that kindness and honesty were the most important things in running a business, more important than profit (I felt a pang of guilt thinking of the bean jar). Honesty and kindness might have been keys for long-term sustainability, but once we were at the bakery, I realized that the real secret, at least for my dad, was determination. That guy was like a machine, the way he moved so quickly from one task to another. And even though he put me on the easy jobs—I couldn't lift the giant bags of flour—I'd be sucking wind by 6:30 a.m., and the only thought in my mind was *Try to make it to 7:00 a.m.* That's when we got a ten-minute coffee-and-doughnut break, and I could listen to Conrad and the other guys talk about what they did the night before.

Incredibly, everyone drank their coffee and ate their doughnuts standing up. I wanted to sit down and rest my legs but didn't dare—there was some kind of silent code that this simply wasn't done.

Coffee break was the time Albert would pass out candy or an apple to each employee while he discreetly took a swig of Seagram's. (One day his swig must have been bigger than usual, because he thought he'd have a piece of candy with it, which later proved to be one of his hearing aid batteries.) I loved this ten-minute break, because it gave me a chance to listen to people from different walks of life, such as ex-con Teddy. My dad believed in giving people a second chance. Couple that with the fact that men were not pounding on the door to work their asses off at 4:00 a.m., and the bakery ended up with more than a few Teddy types.

In later years, I remembered that when I worked at the bakery in my late teens, I gave Teddy a bunch of what I thought was good-natured ribbing. Maybe Teddy didn't see it that way, because after coffee break he motioned for me to come to the back side of the ovens. There he lifted up his T-shirt, pulled out a revolver, and simply said, "It's with me all the time."

Later I mentioned this incident to Conrad, who said, "Be careful, Teddy's more nuts than I am. Three weeks ago Teddy said to me, 'Conrad, you and I are going to knock off a bank. You are going to be the driver. I'll get 70 percent, you'll get 30 percent.'"

They never did rob the bank, so Teddy turned his attention to an easier target. He robbed the bakery!

—~—

After the coffee break it was go, go, go until I ate a sandwich at noon. I noticed my father never stopped to eat lunch; now that I think of it, I didn't see him even drink a glass of water. This despite the fact that with the two industrial-size ovens blasting heat throughout the workday, the temperature inside the bakery during the summer months must have been close to one hundred degrees. But speed was what my father was about, because customers always got the bread the same day it was made.

There were many jobs my father didn't allow me to do because I'd slow down the process. Some of those included pouring all the ingredients into a giant mixer (including those ninety-pound bags of flour), pulling the dough out of the mixer and putting it in giant twelve-foot-long tubs to slowly rise, and later manhandling that same dough from the tubs to the cutting table, where it would be carved into more manageable pieces. Even when I was older, I rarely slid the dough into the ovens, because the oven racks moved faster than I could load them. My tasks were the easier ones, such as bagging bread (I was the only one who wore gloves, because the fresh-from-the-oven bread burned my hands as I put it in the open-ended paper bags), sweeping the floors, arranging dough on trays that would become rolls, and other tasks that didn't involve brute strength or lightning speed.

A frequent job of mine was catching the dough that came out of a machine that rounded it and placing it in wooden boxes, where it would stay until being transferred to the oven. Even that simple job was somewhat of a struggle, because the dough came tumbling out of the machine as fast as I could grab it. I must have looked like Lucy Ricardo and Ethel Mertz in the classic *I Love Lucy* episode where they struggled to keep up with the chocolates coming down the conveyor belt. They were able to eat a few chocolates to save time, but consuming a lump of dough was not an option for me. The rounded dough came out so fast because my father was the one feeding it into the rounder machine. First he would lift a huge slab of dough from one of the tubs onto the cutting table; then, with his Popeye-like forearms bulging, he'd hack off pieces of equal size and hurl each one into the rounder. He was a robot on speed, and after half an hour of struggling to keep up, my arms ached and my legs wobbled. I will admit, he did warn me.

I always marveled that my cousin Steven, just a year older than I, could almost keep up with my dad when we were just fourteen and fifteen years old, respectively. Watching the two of them made me think long and hard about joining the family business when I got older.

Many people who work with a particular kind of food all day long develop a distaste for that food and the smell that goes with it. But I didn't. I loved the aroma of baking bread, and given half a chance, I would have eaten a loaf of French bread while on the job. Instead, I'd bring a loaf home and follow my father's lead by making a big salad sprinkled with olive oil and vinegar and dip the bread crust in the juice. Then I'd immediately go to bed.

When I think back on the bakery of the late 1960s and early 1970s, the color white dominates my image. The walls and ceilings were white, the flour dust that covered the hardwood floors was white, most of the equipment was white, and my father always wore white cotton pants and white T-shirts. The only windows were tiny rectangular ones, spaced irregularly where the wall met the ceiling. Maybe this was to keep employees from taking their eyes off the work, but it also made breaking into the bakery more difficult. And I remember those flour bags stacked atop one another to heights of eight feet. When I was a little kid and Mark and I would visit my father at the bakery, we would scale the flour bags like a mountain, sit on the summit, and observe the hum of activity below us. When Uncle Pons came in from making deliveries, he always came over to us and gave each of us a dollar for coming to work.

Uncle Angelo, however, was another matter; he'd just give us a quick look and not say anything, and Mark and I would shrink back on our mountaintop. I asked my dad why Angelo rarely spoke to me, and Dad said that Angelo was in combat in World War II and probably saw some things that would affect any young man's outlook on the human race. Later, when I was home on college breaks and worked side by side with Angelo while my father was at the dentist, we had some incredibly heated debates about politics. My father got wind of these debates and told me that if I wanted "to keep my job, I had better learn to keep my opinions to myself." That very night I dreamed that the bakery had a new coffee break section like a modern-day Starbucks, where workers could sit outside around little tables with umbrellas. This was where Angelo and I sipped coffee and had heartfelt discussions. I must have smoked some strong weed that night.

Leo was one of my favorite old-timers at the bakery; we often bagged bread side by side and had a chance to talk. We had to raise our voices above the cacophony of clacking and pounding machinery, but because Leo could bag without looking at his hands, he was able to turn his head toward me so I could hear his raspy voice. He'd ask me if was getting any action from girls, and I admitted that whatever action I got was very little. Then he would turn his attention to sports because he was a bookie on the side; my father bought a ticket from him each week, and I always bet on the New York Giants football team. Leo would give me tips about point spreads and how I should be betting on some other teams. I remember saying to my dad that little Leo was one of the sweetest guys I'd ever met. Dad said he'd known him all his life, and, yes, he was sweet. "But don't underestimate him, I saw him throw a wise guy through a plate-glass window for looking at his wife a bit too long." Of course I had to ask Leo about this. "No comment," he said, "but your dad is no pushover. He decked a worker here who gave him lip."

I was shocked. "My dad? Are you sure?"

"Oh, yeah; I needle him about it sometimes, because I know he won't talk about it."

"You mean he feels bad about punching the guy?"

"No, no, no. He feels bad because the guy sued and won 250 dollars."

I was learning a lot at the bakery.

＊

Between the work ethic and honesty of my grandfather Elias and my dad, they set a high standard I knew I'd never live up to. But that was OK, because I gained an appreciation for why my father never came to my soccer games or wrestling matches—after a day at the bakery, he simply had no time or energy. And it's no wonder that if there was a family function on one of his days off, he'd find a way to dance and be the life of the party. It was his way of celebrating having survived another week, and he was going to make the most of it.

CHAPTER ELEVEN

REFLECTING BACK ON MY TEENAGE YEARS, I HAVE FEW REGRETS OVER the things I did, but many concerning those I neglected to do. I wish I had stopped a fight I witnessed or asked a girl out I secretly loved or befriended a kid who seemed to have no friends, and I wish I had asked my father for advice, as it would have led to the dialogue I craved and fewer misunderstandings. But now, as I entered high school, I was carving my own path, and it didn't occur to me that my father had once been a teenager and might have some wisdom to share from the benefit of hindsight. I was too busy exerting my independence and experimenting with new opportunities.

Friends and I were getting drunk on weekends, swilling down Boone's Farm wine and Schlitz beer. I hated the taste of both, particularly those times we'd force ourselves to drink the rotgut in the woods on freezing winter nights—all in an effort to kill brain cells and gain liquid courage so that later in the night, at a high school dance or party, we'd have the nerve to approach girls we liked. And I remember the first time I smoked pot. A bunch of friends were in Cogs's basement; I took a hit, inhaled deeply, and nothing happened. Somebody recommended taking another hit, which I promptly did, and still no high. By the time the grass did its work, I must have taken five deep drags, which was four too many. I first noticed that time slowed down, that I was aware of every word I said, wondering why I said it, and felt the group's eyes on me. My high was the paranoid kind, not the relaxed "let it all hang out" state of mind I was hoping for. Things got worse when I swear I saw Cogs's legs grow by several inches.

You would think I'd never smoke again, but a high schooler's brain is not fully formed, and neither are one's decisions. And so in my freshman and sophomore years of high school, I did plenty of things that didn't make sense or were purely impulsive. One of them was an ill-planned road trip to Maine.

We did not yet have our driver's licenses, so I convinced Opie to hitchhike with me from our homes in Longmeadow, Massachusetts, to coastal Maine. It was summer, and the thought of girls in bikinis at the beach had overtaken the quest to catch big fish and own a cabin.

To make the plan work, I had to lie to my parents that we were taking a bus to Maine. I had looked into the bus trip, but there were so many connections, Opie and I decided we could hitchhike faster—and of course there was the thrill of not following the rules. Hitchhiking back in 1970 was fairly common, but our parents would never have allowed fifteen-year-olds to go that far. But Opie and I had plenty of experience: We had hitchhiked all the way to Ocean City, Maryland, a month earlier, and our parents were none the wiser. Despite a terrible experience, we were more than willing to stick our thumbs—and our necks—out again.

On that Ocean City trip, a man picked us up; Opie got in the front seat and I climbed in the back. We were in the car no more than two minutes when the man put his hand on Opie's thigh. Opie said something to the effect that he was going to get out at the next traffic light. At the light I hopped out of the car from the back seat, but Opie seemed to be struggling with the door. From the outside looking in through the passenger window, I could see Opie's terrified face. I grabbed the door handle and tore it open, allowing Opie to tumble out onto the asphalt just as the man gunned the engine and took off. I helped Opie up from the pavement and asked him what had happened. In a stuttering voice he said the door handle had been removed from his side of the car. Then Opie said, "If you hadn't opened the door from the outside, that guy was going to race away with me in the car when the light changed."

A logical person would never hitchhike again after an experience like that, but Opie and I were anything but logical. We put the experience behind us, or perhaps blocked it out, and we set our sights on Maine. Packing for the trip was easy: a bathing suit, a sleeping bag, a canvas pup tent, and fifteen dollars in cash. We figured we could stay for free at Jane's summer home in Kennebunk (yes, the same Jane from the bungled sixth-grade sleepover). Only now Jane was a friend, who was dating another buddy of mine, nicknamed Busto.

The morning we left on our Maine adventure, we both had our parents fooled that we were taking a bus to Springfield, Massachusetts, and then boarding another bound for Maine. I considered the ruse a little white lie that our parents would never know about. At the outskirts of Longmeadow, we walked down to Interstate 91, stuck out our thumbs, and watched car after car whiz by without slowing down. Maybe our hair had something to do with it: I had a mop of brown curls extending just short of my shoulders, and Opie had long red hair, with ringlets so tight it rose a couple inches straight up from his scalp. At that time, most adults—and they owned the cars—looked down on us young people with long, unruly hair; consequently, we stood with thumbs extended for more than an hour. Finally a Cadillac pulled over and we hopped in, both of us climbing into the back seat. The man at the wheel turned around, shaking his head from side to side with one eyebrow arched. It was Mr. Barger, our friend Booge's father. "What the hell are two cream puffs like you doing on the interstate?"

We explained our plan, and Mr. Barger said we were in luck: He was heading out of town on a business trip and could take us down the Mass Pike as far as Worcester. He gave us a few words of warning but didn't try to talk us out of the trip, probably because his generation had hitchhiked even more than ours. I liked Mr. Barger, and liked how I often saw him at his home reading the newspaper at the kitchen table. He'd welcome me, motion for me to sit across from him, ask a few questions, then mostly listen and nod. I knew when the conversation was over, because he'd simply go back to reading the paper. I don't think he ever met my dad or Opie's dad, but they were similar in that all were hardworking, providing for our every need, but somewhat hands-off when it came to "parenting." They were nothing like the helicopter parents of today. I don't recall seeing any of them at our sporting events, getting involved with our homework, or prying into our personal lives. They were simply steady men, grinding it out as a baker, salesman, and supermarket manager. But in their own ways, my friends' fathers did have an influence on me by demonstrating the value of reliability, good humor, and stability.

If my friends' dads knew I was usually the ringleader of the adventures that got their sons in trouble, they didn't let on, because they never lectured me. I guess they accepted me warts and all, and figured their boys were old enough to choose their friends. And now, with

Mr. Barger driving us away from Longmeadow, I had the feeling he wouldn't squeal on us.

Our trip was off to a good start, and our luck held—several other kind drivers gave us lifts, and we made it to Kennebunk that night. It was a long day to be sure, more than twelve hours of hitchhiking and riding (yes, the bus would have been faster), but we still had our fifteen dollars each to spend. We showed up at Jane's house just before midnight, and her mother let us in.

It's hard to imagine a world without cell phones—Jane and her mother only knew we were due sometime that day or the next. They were genuinely happy to see us, didn't make a big deal about the late hour, but simply rolled with the situation, fixing us something to eat and asking about our plans. Later we pitched our tent in their side yard under a big oak. Calling it a tent is generous, as the damn thing was more like a canvas coffin and must have been designed for little kids. It had a pervasive moldy smell, strong enough that you could taste it. The sides sagged so much that the stinking canvas was just inches from our faces when we lay down. Our feet stuck out the opening when we lay down inside with our shoulders touching. Yet we felt lucky. We were in Maine, and tomorrow we would be at the beach, with adventures stretching out before us.

Ah, the innocence of youth. If we had known what was in store for us, we would have asked Jane's mother to roll us up in the tent and load it on the next bus home.

Does the ocean ever warm up in Maine? No. But we had traveled far, and we were going in. It was early morning with just a couple sunbathers on the beach. The waves rolling in were moderate and looked perfect for bodysurfing. And so on the count of three, Opie and I raced into the sea, where the cold promptly took our breath away. The waves, however, gave us good rides, and somehow we ignored the pleas of our skinny little bodies and focused on who could catch the longest ride. After surfing five or six waves, we could no longer ignore the numbing effect of the frigid water and decided to head in. The ocean had other ideas.

I didn't know what a riptide was, but I realized I wasn't making any progress toward the beach no matter how hard I stroked. Opie was just four or five feet away from me, and he too was swimming for all he was worth. The shore looked far away, well, because it was. It hit me that we were at least a hundred feet farther out than where we had been bodysurfing just a minute earlier. That gave me a jolt of fear-induced adrenaline, and I renewed my kicking and stroking with the vigor of an Olympian in a race. And it did seem like a race, a race for my life. If only I had known that fighting against a riptide is exactly the wrong thing to do.

I paused to catch my breath, and Opie did the same. He was still next to me, and when our eyes met it reminded me of the terror I saw on his face through the passenger window of the pervert's car. Only this time, there was nothing I could do to help him.

I started swimming again, but like on a treadmill, it didn't matter how hard I tried; forward progress just wasn't happening. My arms gave out first, each one feeling like a water-soaked log. I was unable to lift them, so I switched to the breast stroke.

We're being swept out to sea, and no one is going to miss us for hours, I realized.

Why we didn't shout for help, I'll never know. I wouldn't be the first person in a drowning situation who didn't cry out. Maybe it's embarrassment for being so stupid, maybe you are so focused on swimming you forget, or maybe you don't dare stop your strokes long enough to gather a lungful of air and holler *Help!*

"Toug," I heard Opie gasp, "I can't . . . swim anymore."

He was behind me now. I glanced over my shoulder, and I could only see the top of his red hair. It was one of the most sickening feelings I've ever experienced—both of us together, and neither one could help the other. The only words I could croak out were "Keep trying."

I kept kicking with my legs and breaststroking with my arms, struggling to keep my head above a thin layer of foam. What happened next seems nothing short of a miracle. I felt the current release me, and just seconds later one of my feet scraped sand.

Opie was now several yards behind me, and I heard a plea: "Toug, help; I'm not going to make it."

"You can do it!" I screamed.

A wave pushed me over and I took in a mouthful of water. But at least I was propelled toward shore, and now both my feet briefly touched sand in between the crests of the waves.

Opie was dog-paddling, and a wave slammed his head forward and under. Then the next wave pushed him toward me. His head was back up, and his eyes were like saucers as he panted. It was awful. I had nothing left, just a feeling like I was in a straitjacket, unable to lift my leaden arms.

I let the next wave carry me, and I could now stand on the bottom. When I looked back for Opie, I couldn't see him. I was close to tears and filled with a dread the likes of which I pray I never experience again.

Then I saw him, just a few yards to my left. He was standing too. The next wave knocked us both down, but the water was shallow; we crawled our way up to the beach, feeling heavy and stiff. Once out of the water, we just sat. When I got my breath back, all I could say was "I thought we were goners." Then we staggered up the shore to where we had left the towels Jane let us borrow and collapsed on them, shivering but thankful for the sun.

Our actions in the riptide were all wrong. Instead of exhausting yourself fighting the current to head directly toward shore, a person should focus on conserving strength. A riptide forms at a dip between two sandbars where outflowing water will pull a swimmer with it. Usually both the dip and rip are relatively narrow. If caught in a riptide, let it carry you until the current slackens. Then swim parallel to the beach and out of the current. That way you will have some energy to slowly make your way back to the beach. But trust me when I say it takes willpower to stay calm and not frantically swim for shore the minute you realize the current has you in its clutches. Many years later, while I was swimming alone at Puerto Rico's Playa Jobos, I was caught once again. While my mind knew what to do, every instinct in my body was screaming for me to swim for shore.

I'm glad that scare at the rip in Kennebunk did not taint my love affair with water, because rivers, lakes, and oceans have brought me so much joy, and I feel at home when swimming in them. A friend said I was part otter, and often that's exactly how I feel. I can't think of any other thing that makes me feel so alive. I could be having an absolutely miserable day, but going for a swim can change my mood in an instant. I call water the "total mood changer." Jump in a lake on a warm day, and see if you agree.

Looking back, I'm glad I had that scare in the riptide, because maybe I was getting a little too comfortable in the water, a little too cocky about my swimming ability. While I might love the ocean, I learned it can turn on you in a second. And a couple years later the message was hammered home again by a river that I took too lightly and didn't respect its power. I would also soon learn that people could be similar—they could change in ways you never saw coming.

The rest of our visit to Kennebunk was either uneventful or overshadowed in my memory by the riptide. But I'd certainly remember if there were bikini-clad girls eager to meet two intrepid travelers, and that never happened. More important, Opie and I were alive after our close call, and quite fortunate we didn't wash up somewhere on the coast of France. The smart thing to do would have been to head back home and not push our luck. Instead we hitchhiked farther up the coast.

Our next stop was to see my friend Andrea, who summered on Squirrel Island. We spent a couple days enjoying the island, but the only event I clearly recall was an evening party open to all the islanders. Somehow Opie and I acquired many beers and a joint and, in the course of the night, became separated. I became lost as I tried to navigate my way back to our tent at Andrea's house and ended up taking a rest on some rocks by the ocean. Tired from all the walking and wandering, my eye fell on a patch of sand between two boulders. I lay down on the sand and listened to the gentle lapping of waves just a few feet away. Stars stretched endlessly above, and as I scanned them I wondered where my life was heading. It seemed to me that all I did was bounce from place to place, always either in the woods or on the water, searching for something new and different. Then I promptly fell asleep. A couple hours later I was shaken awake by Opie. "Toug, the waves are lapping at your feet. You were about to be taken out by the high tide. I searched the whole island for you, and now I have to rescue you from being taken out to sea."

I looked up at him groggily, not sure where I was. At first I thought we were still back in Kennebunk. Then the night slowly came into focus and I remembered getting lost.

"Did you find any girls?" I asked.

"Naw, but that should be the least of your worries. You really were about to find yourself in a pickle with high tide coming."

He was right about the tide rising. With Opie holding my arm, I struggled to my feet. I was glad he had found me; it would have been a cold and miserable night huddling on those rocks until dawn. I was about to thank Opie when he said, "Glad I could be of service. But, gee, I remember shouting for your help in the riptide, and all I heard was 'You can do it!'"

———

And so our big trip to Maine ended with us hung over and hitchhiking home, no conquests of bikini-clad girls to brag about. But just two months later I did have my first sexual encounter, with a pretty girl from my English class during a teacher-chaperoned camping trip. The class had just read Thoreau's *Walden*, and the teacher—God bless him for the effort—organized a camping trip for the weekend where the class was to "live simply and think of some of Thoreau's teachings." One student's parents owned a few acres of wooded hillside up in the Berkshires, and that's where the class was headed.

For some reason, myself and a buddy, John, could not go on the first night, a Friday, but we were able to have my mother drop us off Saturday afternoon. Our instructions from the teacher were only to bring a tent, a sleeping bag, matches, and some food. But since John and I were coming on our own, I figured I could break that rule and the teacher would never know. I smuggled a few beers into my pack, along with a portable radio and a lantern.

Once at the land in the Berkshires, we walked up to the teacher's campsite, which was all on its own in a little meadow, away from where the main body of kids had pitched their tents up near the hilltop. My teacher hadn't even brought a tent but instead had a made a lean-to out of hemlock boughs. We exchanged a few greetings, and he asked us to try to honor the spirit of Thoreau by uncluttering the mind and spending time in quiet reflection without modern-day distractions. John and I assured him that we would. As we were leaving, I noticed his plate of half-eaten dinner. All that was on it was the picked-over backbone of a trout and some greens.

"Did you catch that trout here?" I asked.

"Yup; there's a stream at the base of the hill. I'm trying to keep it simple like Thoreau."

I was impressed that my English teacher had managed to catch his dinner, but the trout skeleton hardly looked appealing.

When we reached our classmates and unpacked our radio and beer, we were treated like conquering heroes. While I liked parts of Thoreau's *Walden*, particularly how old Henry built his cabin on the pond for something like fifty bucks, much of the rest of his book was above my reading level and, for that matter, beyond my comprehension. Apparently the other students felt the same way, because they had no qualms about passing around the beer and listening to the radio. We spent the evening talking by a big fire, and John and I stayed up until everyone else had gone to sleep. When I finally crawled into my sleeping bag inside my tent, I got quite a surprise. A pretty girl from my class was already snuggled up inside the bag. And she was stark naked!

To say that I didn't know what I was doing when I slipped inside the sleeping bag next to her is an understatement. All I remember is kissing and rubbing parts of her body. Most of the time I didn't know what I was rubbing. Junior high and high school in the late 1960s and early 1970s certainly didn't have sex education classes, and my parents never discussed the birds and bees. However, my mother did allow me to read the book *For Boys Only*, so I knew a couple basics.

Those basics didn't do me any good that night, because both the girl and I, at fourteen and fifteen years of age, respectively, were not ready for sex. Thankfully, we fell asleep tangled in each other's arms.

The next morning when we were all packed up and hiking down the hill, I went by the teacher, who, true to his word, was reading Thoreau by the cold ashes of his little fire pit. I was glad he was camped down here so that he didn't know about the night's activities. But then he said, "Mr. Tougias. I don't know exactly what went on up there last night, but there better not be any surprises in nine months."

I swallowed, but no words came out, so I kept walking. *How did he know???*

———

Looking back, I wished I had asked that girl to go steady with me, but for one reason or another I never did, and we lost track of each other. Maybe I was a little afraid of her. After all, I wasn't the brightest bulb in the pack. In my junior high yearbook, another girl had written, "Michael, we've been great friends for a long time—now let's try something more exciting." I was either too dense to take her up on her offer or too intimidated by her bold approach. No, I had to lust after girls who were harder to get, or fantasize about older women.

There was one pretty housewife who made a habit of lying out in her yard in a bikini every time I mowed her lawn. I had a hunch she was toying with me, teasing me for her own reasons, but I simply didn't know for sure. She might have been waiting for me to make the first move, which terrified me. So instead I fantasized while she continually shifted position on the chaise lounge in her backyard. It sure took me a long time to cut her lawn while stealing glances at her and hoping she'd make the first move—or at the very least slip out of her bikini.

This young housewife often had me over for jobs so small she could have done them herself in two minutes. She always made me lemonade, and when she paid me she'd ask me about school and what I was doing for fun. But unlike Dustin Hoffman in *The Graduate*, I never got up the courage to seal the deal. A couple years later, when my hormones rocketed into the stratosphere and I was ready for action, she and her husband moved and I kicked myself.

Cutting lawns, shoveling snow, working at the bakery on occasion, and delivering newspapers were just a few of my many sources of income during my high school years. I guess some of my dad's work ethic had rubbed off on me. By sophomore year I landed a job at a supermarket, where I worked with Opie and Dale and new friends from the neighboring town. I loved the camaraderie, getting to know repeat customers, and a regular paycheck. On the flip side, the owner of the store was a self-important jerk, a few customers were rude and petty, and the pay was minimum wage. But by working at the supermarket, I got an education that no amount of schooling could ever provide, and by juggling work with school and sports, I became proficient at time management.

Because I worked hard, I didn't spend the money I made foolishly, saving most of it. In the back of my mind, I still thought about buying a cabin.

CHAPTER TWELVE

My aunt recently told me that when I was "acting wild," my mother would break down in tears and say, "I don't know what to do with him." I think that contributed greatly to the divide between my father and me. He thought I was taking advantage of my mother, ignoring her warnings, admonishments, and instructions, which sometimes left her in a fragile, depressed mood when he got home from the bakery. That in turn caused him to lash out at me, and neither one of us had the sense to sit down and try to explain our point of view. I can now see that I was inadvertently causing his relationship with my mother to suffer, but at the time I was blind to those kind of ramifications.

During my high school years, I did give my mom some relief. I was rarely home, which allowed her peace; just as important, much of the news from school was good. My grades were slowly inching upward, I was involved in sports, and I was even elected to the student council.

Freshman year, however, was an eye-opener. The Vietnam War was still on everyone's mind, and all of us male students wore our hair long either in an act of defiance or simply to keep up with the prevailing style. Teenagers wanted to express themselves, but my high school had a dress code that mandated the boys must wear ties. Older students had had enough of that rule, and my earliest memory of freshman year was when a senior demanded I take off my tie, hand it to him, and follow him, which I did. He led me to the courtyard of the school, where a crowd of students had started a small fire. The senior threw my tie into the flames. It was like being welcomed to the big leagues. These older guys were serious—and who could blame them. They were likely to be drafted, and a low draft lottery number could mean a one-way ticket to Southeast Asia. "Tricky Dick" Nixon still used his heavy hand to stop protesters. (That same year, police, army soldiers, and marines stopped antiwar protesters in Washington, DC, by arresting every demonstrator who marched on the Capitol, arresting and herding seven thousand protesters into the DC jail, football field, and coliseum.)

Even though my father and I often watched the TV news about Vietnam at the same time, we never had a deep discussion. I did hear him say once, and only once, that we should either fight to win or not at all. And I know he heard me say I'd rather move to Canada than go to Vietnam, but he didn't respond. This was a man who absolutely loved his military service in 1945–47, still kept his uniform and helmet, and talked fondly of both his war buddies and his officers. He must have been conflicted about both the Vietnam War and my comment about leaving the country to avoid it.

<hr />

Another poignant memory from that period involved my sister, Lynn, who was a senior when I was a freshman. I had joined the wrestling team and was selected to be in a tournament. Lynn was in the bleachers, as were many other students. When my match was called, I walked out on the mats, adrenaline pumping through me. I was a good wrestler, and in this sport my small size was no obstacle. I'd be matched against a wrestler in the same weight class—the whopping 104-pound class. In junior high I had made it to the finals of a tournament, easily winning match after match, but on the day of the finals I had the flu and had to forfeit the potential championship. Now I was ready for redemption.

My opponent was a tall wiry kid from the Quabbin region of Massachusetts who was just as fit as I was. I scored a takedown in the first period, accumulated more points in the second, and neither one of us could do much damage in the third period. I remember my mouth was pasty and felt like it was filled with cotton, making it hard to breathe. I had expended every ounce of strength in my little body and, judging from his gasps, thought my opponent had done the same. My point total was something like six and his was zero, and all I had to do was hang on and not do anything dumb. I must have let my guard down—or maybe I didn't have the energy to even fight defensively—because with just thirty seconds left, this kid flipped me over, pinned me, and won the match.

When I came home that afternoon, I could not have been any lower. Lynn, in an attempt to lift my spirits, said, "You fought a good match."

But I was so down on myself, I thought she was being sarcastic and said something like "F— you!" Hearing this, my mother came into the kitchen. Lynn said, "I was only trying to tell him that I saw how hard he fought." But I wasn't listening and stormed down to my room in the finished basement. I never did apologize to Lynn; the sting of the loss was just too much to bring up the subject.

I'm sure Lynn told my father about my wrestling match, and I waited for him to offer some consoling words. But my guess is that he knew I was hurting, didn't want to reopen the wound, and figured I'd bring up the subject if I needed to talk. And so, like so many other times, we missed an opportunity, carefully avoiding the elephant in the room.

I never lost another match that year, but it didn't matter; losing that match in the final seconds tainted me. I found myself conserving strength during matches so that I'd never lose in the final seconds again. In wrestling you need confidence, and sometimes it's best to go all out and try to pin your opponent as quickly as possible.

Wrestling is a lonely sport. Although you are part of a team, when the whistle blows it's just you and your opponent on the mat, with small crowds cheering either for you or against you. I longed to play a sport like basketball, where players pass to one another and work in sync on the court toward a common goal. But I was much too small for basketball and wasn't very good at it. Wrestling and boxing were sports I was good at, but they simply were not fun. To make matters worse, my wrestling coach had no joy, no sense of humor, and kept us in line with the stick and never the carrot. I remember when the coach had me fight a senior and I was losing. He shouted, "Mike, you're looking at the ceiling." I wish I had had the balls to say, "No shit, Sherlock."

The experience taught me a lot. Later in life, I coached my son's basketball team, and I made a real effort to make the least-accomplished players on the team feel good about themselves and know that they were important to the team. That approach worked well: Each year we had a winning record, and kids on the team were not shy about sharing their ideas of how we could get better.

I rejoined the wrestling team my sophomore year, but now I was aware of the toll wrestling was taking not only on me (the tension the day of each match was making me a nervous wreck) but also on my fellow wrestlers. Opie was one of them, and during a scrimmage he was thrown so hard on the mat I swear I heard a terrible crack. He had landed on his tailbone and let out a shriek and then didn't move. I thought his back was broken.

Opie fully recovered, but if he wrestled again, it wasn't for long. Other wrestlers were trying to stay in their weight classes by jumping rope next to the school's red-hot basement boiler—while wearing rubber suits! These guys were fifteen to seventeen years old, a time when they should be growing and putting on weight! Back in the early 1970s it was rare for a teenager to be overweight. Every one of my friends was rail-thin, and when we took our shirts off, you could see our rib cages. Most kids were so active, they burned off calories faster than they could consume them. And yet some of these wrestlers were both starving themselves and exercising in ways that were downright dangerous.

By the end of sophomore year, I'd had enough of the grind and told the coach I wasn't coming back next year. He asked why, and I just shrugged. How do you tell an adult their leadership is all wrong?

The other sport I played was soccer, and I was awful: Slow afoot, and shorter than everyone else, my kicks were about as powerful as a five-year-old's. I was still on the junior varsity team when I was a junior, and the other players elected me co-captain, probably because I was a grade ahead of many of them. Similar to the wrestling coach, the soccer coach too was a stern taskmaster who cared more about winning than developing players or making sure they had fun. As co-captain, before the start of each game I'd trot out to center field to meet the refs and the opposing student captain then head back to the bench. And that's where I stayed. This coach, who probably thought he should be leading a World Cup team, almost never put me in the game. Friends of mine made matters worse by standing behind the bench and shouting "Put Toug in!" I'm sure that just made the coach stick to his guns and keep me seated.

It didn't help my soccer career that I was extremely flat-footed, with a bone protruding where my arch should have been. Sometimes after practice my socks would be bloody from my deformed feet rubbing the sides of my cleats. Yet I stayed on the team because, unlike wrestling, I felt part of the team and wanted to be with friends. Some coaches and parents never seem to understand that many students who play sports are doing it for the social interaction rather than for the competition. Kids just want to be part of a group, and I was no exception.

❦

My relationship with my father improved on some fronts and tanked on others. He was delighted when I brought home a report card with improved grades and said something like "Not bad for the son of a son of an immigrant." But a couple weeks later he was furious when the school informed him I'd be serving several weeks' detention for a variety of disruptions, including uncontrolled, nonstop laughter. He wouldn't listen to why I was disruptive, and he certainly didn't want to hear about continuously laughing in class. But in my defense, most people would have lost it when my friend Andy, fresh back from a trip to Spain, was invited by our Spanish teacher to give a slideshow about his travels.

Andy was quite proud of his photography and seemed to enjoy being the "teacher for a day." About halfway through his presentation, one of the slides became blurry. I watched as if I were high on pot: The images in the photo changed shape; colors merged. It was a psychedelic show of the first order, and it occurred so slowly that few of us grasped that the slide was actually melting from the overheating bulb. I clapped my hands in appreciation of Andy's unusual presentation, and other students joined in and cheered. Then Andy, who was standing next to the projector, said, "I smell smoke." A second later, the entire plastic carousel housing all his precious slides went up in flames. Our teacher, Miss Simmons, let out a shriek and ran for help. Andy frantically searched the room for a fire extinguisher, while I shouted for him to take his shirt off and extinguish the flames. He called me an idiot and suggested I use my own shirt. Other kids chimed in with advice, and most of us moved away from the projector.

As suddenly as the fire started, it went out on its own. When Miss Simmons returned with two other teachers, we students were all chanting "Andy! Andy! Andy!" in appreciation of his diversionary and revolutionary use of slides. Then I got the giggles and Miss Simmons lost her cool and said, "Shut up." For some reason that only made me laugh harder, and the whole class joined in. And that, dear reader, is how I found myself in the assistant principal's office with a week's detention and note for my parents to sign and return.

While I tried to explain the burning slide carousel incident to my father (he was in no mood to hear the story), I did not tell him about a more serious incident—when a guidance counselor tried to engage me in inappropriate sexual conversation. The episode began when the editor of the school newspaper asked me if the guidance department had been helpful to me and I responded, in typical blunt "Mike" fashion, "Not at all." When the paper came out, I was called into the guidance department. A male counselor asked me why I had negative things to say about his department. I gave some short, lame answer. We talked a bit, and then the counselor suddenly switched topics. His next question to me was if I'd ever seen two men performing a certain sexual act on each other. I sat there frozen, wondering if I had heard his question correctly. Then he continued, describing the sex act in detail. When you're a freshman and a person in authority does something strange, your instinct is to freeze. When he finally finished his strange lecture and I had not said a word, he asked if I had anything I wanted to talk about. I said no, and he dismissed me by bringing the conversation back to how the guidance department could help students in many ways. Maybe in today's world, a student would immediately tell their parents what happened, but in 1970 the only person I told was Opie.

Perhaps the incident with the guidance counselor was why I never sought out any teachers as mentors in high school. It was a missed opportunity I'd regret for the rest of my life, because later, when it came to applying to and choosing a college, I could have benefited from the advice of someone with perspective on my strengths and on my future. Neither my father nor my mother attended college, or had the luxury of picking a profession, so when college application time rolled around, the three of us stumbled through the process. That's not to say I didn't have mentors. Both my parents played that role, imparting and demonstrating priceless qualities, particularly character and integrity. Those two traits can't be taught, but they can be observed and, if you're perceptive, emulated. But that realization comes later, usually well after your teens.

While my father was often mad at me for what was going on at school (and later with the police), my resentment of his control over me reached its peak that freshman year of high school when he intervened in a fistfight I was about to begin. A group of neighborhood kids were playing Monopoly on our picnic table, and toward the end of the game, there were just me and a neighbor who was a couple years older than I left on the board. When he knew the odds were clearly in my favor to win, he suddenly tipped the board over and said, "Game's over!" Something snapped in me, and I lunged for him. He escaped and ran around our house, with me behind him screaming, "I'm going to kill you!" Just as I had him cornered by our porch, my father came running out of the house and pulled me off him. I hadn't even landed a punch. My father had me in a bear hug and dragged me into the house, as if I had done something wrong rather than the real criminal who had tipped over the Monopoly board.

I've never been so filled with rage in my life, and I tried to explain what had happened. My father cut me off and said I couldn't go around fighting neighbors over a game. Another misunderstanding between father and son. Now I can understand that he had to stop the fight, but at the time I was furious. I couldn't articulate my frustration, and he couldn't explain his duty as a parent. So much of life is spent never knowing the other person's intent because all we have are words, and they seem to abandon us when emotions are at the boiling point.

My refuge from frustrations with school, my coaches, and my father came in two very different forms: alcohol and the outdoors. As I mentioned earlier, alcohol was liquid courage, and I don't remember drinking it for pleasure or because it tasted good. And the pot I smoked had no real benefits either; I was only doing what my friends were doing, never thinking about the why. Thank God there was no cocaine, opioids, or LSD readily available, because the Mike of the early 1970s seemed to live by the motto of "Go for it." Today when I see a young person hooked on one of these drugs, I try not to judge them but instead remember what I was like in my younger seasons.

Although the drinking age was eighteen at the time, we never had much trouble scoring beer or wine and occasionally hard liquor. Countless times I simply stood outside a package store (in our little world of Massachusetts, that's what we called liquor stores) and waited until someone under thirty, always a male, was heading inside. I'd ask, "Can you buy a six-pack for me?" and about a quarter of the people said "Sure," and I handed them the money. It was that easy. I'm glad it's a bit tougher today.

Luckily, my interest in the outdoors still asserted itself now and then, and more than once I'd round up Opie, Cogs, Dale, and Booge for a trip to the Meadows, where fishing was the objective rather than getting drunk. We were neither jocks nor brains nor hoods, but roamers always looking for a new adventure. I can still see the group of us on our bikes, fishing rods across the handlebars, gliding downhill from Longmeadow Street toward the floodplain of the Meadows. We had to cross train tracks, and invariably we stopped and laid pennies on the tracks if we saw a train coming. Then we'd scramble to the side of the tracks and cover our ears as the deafening roar of the train shook the earth, flattening our pennies into three times their normal size. I once put a religious medal on the tracks and later fell into a daylong despair, thinking I'd go straight to hell. I didn't tell my mother, a strict Catholic, because she likely would have stayed up all night praying and worrying about me and then drag me to Novena (a service on Mondays) for the next year.

Often our little posse would stop at Longmeadow Brook, not far from where Opie caught that giant rainbow trout several years earlier. In the spring, sea lampreys would migrate from the ocean, come up the Connecticut River, and then enter our brook to spawn. While they resemble eels, lampreys are a jawless fish with a large round mouth that includes circular rows of tiny teeth. The lamprey latches onto a fish with this suction cup–like mouth and then sucks its blood. We viewed them as disgusting, evil serpents that must be destroyed before they latched onto our beloved trout. The fact that lampreys had been coming up Longmeadow Brook for eons, and were more intent on breeding than eating, never entered our consciousness. We didn't realize they were as much a part of the ecosystem as the trout, and that various fish and birds ate young lampreys. Instead we viewed ourselves as knights in shining armor, defending our stream against these dastardly cowards. That, however, is not exactly how it all worked out.

My first encounter with a lamprey occurred when I was crossing the brook. I had taken off my sneakers to keep them dry, and one of my steps landed directly on a lamprey. The creature immediately wrapped its body around my ankle as I screamed bloody murder and did a frantic kind of Irish jig to shake it free. The lamprey darted away, and I not only charged to shore but didn't stop until I was a good ten feet from the stream, hyperventilating. I have no idea how big the lamprey was, but later when I saw a few more, they ranged in size from two to three feet.

When I told Dale about the incident, he relayed a story that topped mine, explaining how he'd had an encounter while walking along nearby Mill Brook. Dale wasn't trout fishing but instead was looking for six-packs of beer that older kids had stashed in the stream to keep cold. He had spotted a single beer at the bottom of the stream and shimmied out on a branch to retrieve it. The branch cracked and slowly started to sag toward the water, and Dale put his hand out to keep from getting dropped in the stream. His hand hit a lamprey, and it curled around his wrist, leaving him with the unenviable choice of removing his hand and getting fully dunked into the stream or keeping the lamprey pinned under his hand while he repositioned his legs to try and shimmy back off the branch. With a moving lamprey on his arm, he never fully had time to weigh his options but instead let out a scream and fell into the brook.

Dale and I told the others about our experiences, and we went on a lamprey hunt. You would think we would use steel-tipped trident spears if we were serious, but instead our weapons of choice were croquet mallets, probably because that's what we found in Booge's garage before we started on our daring mission. (I think I was the only one who seriously hoped to find a lamprey; the others came along for the possibility of finding beer.) When we got to the stream, Booge led the way, using his mallet as a walking stick in the knee-deep water, the rest of us trailing behind, shoulder to shoulder, covering the stream from bank to bank.

Booge entered a deep pool and asked, "What if a lamprey latches onto my leg and starts sucking my blood?"

"Don't be an idiot," I said, annoyed that he put the thought in my head. "They go after fish."

"I don't know about that," someone interjected. "They might attack one of us any minute, and we're not going to get them off with a croquet mallet."

Dale asked, "Do lampreys have eyes?"

"Of course they do," I snapped. But I really had no idea.

Booge turned back and looked at me. "Well, the one that wrapped around your ankle didn't see so well. I think . . ." Then Booge screamed, "Lamprey!" That's when our carefully planned lamprey hunt fell apart. We all started swearing and smashing the water with our croquet mallets, water spraying in all directions.

I never actually spotted the lamprey, and for all I know, maybe Booge saw a tree root, but we smashed the water into a froth. One of us hollered "Halt!" as if we were in combat and needed to cease fire before we killed one another.

A silence fell over the stream.

"We showed that bastard," I offered. "Sure gave him a good pounding."

"So where is it?" wondered Booge.

Dale made the suggestion first that we all followed: "I don't give a rat's ass. I'm getting out of this brook. Let's call it a day."

That night I told my father about all the dangers I had faced in the Meadows: monstrous lampreys, giant snapping turtles, and enormous snakes. He responded with a commonsense question: "Well, then why keep going there?"

How could I not? It was in my DNA that places like the Meadows would lure me in, and they still do today.

———

One spring there was flooding throughout the Meadows, and the Connecticut River sent its brown waters groping for hollows and depressions to fill. With the river water came its fish. When the river receded, I'm sure most of the fish went with it, but some very large fish were left stranded in small pools. As they rooted and foraged for food on the bottom, they sent up swirls of mud, which in turn attracted us like magnets. We had been fishing in the Meadows long enough to suspect they were carp, a "trash fish" not for the sportsman and belittled as a food source.

They don't have the beauty of a trout but instead are rather ugly, with a drooping mouth and fat body covered in armor-like scales. The important thing to us, however, was their size, and we could tell that the ones in the tiny pond we visited were about two feet long.

We tried to catch them with hooks baited with worms or corn, but for some reason these fish were not in a biting mood. Only Booge had a bite, and the fish snapped his line when it surged away. After several hours, our frustration was at a fever pitch. We had glimpses of these monsters when they swirled and their backs came out of the water, but try as we might we could not catch them. We were fishless but not defeated, vowing to come back the next day better equipped.

That night when I closed my eyes in bed, I saw those brown swirls. (Little has changed at age sixty-five. Whenever I fish the Brewster Flats when stripers are prowling, I see their black shadows against the light sand as soon as I lie down to sleep.) In the morning I replaced my light line with twenty-pound-test monofilament, and I brought weighted treble hooks used for ocean fishing. Back at our mudhole, Opie took the first cast, sending his treble hook so far it sailed across the pond and into the brush. I burst out laughing, but promptly slipped on the muddy bank. Skidding down the mud, my ass ended up in the pond, and Opie, Cogs, and Dale had a good laugh. Covered in muck, I took my shirt and shoes off. Luckily, it was a hot sultry day, the air steaming and pungent with the smell of the swamp, and I felt quite at home in my mud-splattered state. Dale said I looked like a skinny, wimpy version of the Creature from the Black Lagoon.

We all continued casting. Every now and then our treble hooks would bump into a carp, and the fish would boil on the surface before gliding away. We'd reel our hooks back, and often there was a fish scale attached, about the size of a quarter.

After about half an hour, one of my casts hooked into a carp and off it went to the races, the drag on my old Mitchel 300 reel screaming. When I applied some leverage, I lost my balance and found myself sitting in the mud. One of my friends helped me up and grabbed the back of my belt so I wouldn't fall again, steadying me as I fought the fish. The Three Stooges had nothing on us. The carp never jumped but instead went in

THE WATERS BETWEEN US

circles around the tiny pond. Every now and then I thought it broke free because the line stopped moving and we couldn't see the fish, but then the reeds would sway where the carp had stopped to regain its strength before making its next loop. After five or ten minutes we had the carp onshore, and I estimated its weight at ten to fifteen pounds.

That night I told my father and Mark about the fish, and how we were deep in the jungles of the Meadows, where we discovered this unknown enchanting pond with big fish trapped in it. However, I recently looked at two photos from that day and realized I was certainly exaggerating. One photo is of me holding the carp; the other is of Booge and Dale looking into the murky water. They are dressed in blue jeans with their shirts off, ribs sticking out, hands on hips. We weren't exactly out in the wild slaying these monsters, because in the background of that picture are two rusty oil drums sticking out of the pond and the highway, Interstate 91, towering above us.

Me at age three. In most pictures of me from age three to ten I'm holding either a toy tomahawk, knife, or gun. Guess I was practicing to be a mountain man.

You can see the excitement on my face while my father holds the bass we caught on Lake Morey. Note that I was probably too chicken to handle the fish myself.

Mark and me with our early morning stringer of fish.
I'm playing the part of the proud older brother.

From left to right:
Mark, Lynn, Bob, and me.

My father was a sergeant in the US Army and served at the tail end of WWII.

Dad, Lynn, and Mom at Lynn's high school graduation.

Dad as American Revolution Minuteman. He loved history.

Don't mess with wildlife. This shot was taken right before the moose charged.

From left to right: Dale, Opie, Booge (standing), me, Cogs.

The Winooski River Raft Race was dangerous one year because of high water, and so was my raft ride down the Huntington River.

The cabin when I bought it in 1979.

The cabin deck—the one place I can sit for hours.

The cabin today with Booge and Cogs.

The cabin today. My daughter Kristin and I.

Enjoying the pond at the cabin.

View from the cabin deck.

CHAPTER THIRTEEN

When we were at the carp pond, I never even noticed there were a couple oil drums in the water. That was an indication of how little protection wetlands and rivers had prior to the Clean Water Act of 1972. This environmental law was a game changer, and our waterways slowly began to heal. No longer did we have to read about such events as the Cuyahoga River in Cleveland catching fire because of the pollutants that had been dumped in it. And for me personally, this was the time I started having serious concerns about the way we treated our natural places and how only the federal government could right the wrongs inflicted on our waterways since the beginning of the industrial revolution. I also formed the opinion that human population growth would soon be unsustainable if we wanted a healthy planet. (And this was in the early 1970s, when the population was only half of what it is today!) So many of the world's problems seemed to be exacerbated by humans covering the planet like rats, and few politicians ever acknowledged the threat. Paul Ehrlich's book *The Population Bomb* had a profound impact on me, and while the calamities predicted did not immediately materialize, I figured they were surely coming down the road unless we changed our ways.

I began reading the newspaper on a regular basis, and with my new-found interest in worldwide matters, my interest in schoolwork, particularly history, social studies, and English, ramped up. My grades continued to climb, my impulsive behavior decreased, and a détente with my dad replaced our headbutting. Life at home was good, maybe because I was almost never there. Lynn was off to college, and my father took over as our household Beatles fan, listening to "My Sweet Lord," "Let It Be," and "The Long and Winding Road." Some of that music and artistic creativity surely rubbed off on Mark, as he pursued playing the guitar and oil painting. My mother now combined homemaking with volunteer work. Bob, who was several years younger than I, showed the same interest Mark and I did in the natural world.

I began passing along what I had learned about fishing to Bob and took him to the annual Fishing Derby at Laurel Park. It wasn't exactly angling in Montana but more like fishing in a bathtub. This tiny pond had been stocked with trout, and on derby day it was ringed with kids armed with rods, nets, vests, and hats pierced with dangling lures. When the gun went off, designating the start of the derby, one hundred kids cast lures or worms all at once. Some casts went clear across the pond and hooked young anglers on the opposite bank. Most of us found our lines tangled into a mess. Despite the chaos, we managed to catch a couple trout (that had probably been starved at the hatchery the week before the contest), and Bob was a quick learner. Later that spring, Bob and I went to a lake, and to help increase his odds of catching a largemouth bass, I first went in with mask and snorkel to scout things out. Near a sunken log I saw two big bass. I motioned Bob to come down the shore my way and pointed to the spot where he should cast. I submerged, saw his lure hit the water and the bass grab it, and then enjoyed the battle from the fish's perspective. Bob landed the bass and then let it go, and all three of us (I'm assuming the bass was happy to be free) were in a fine mood.

My parents, noting my newfound responsibility, offered to take us to Moosehead Lake, where we boys had been begging to go since we first learned about the great fishing there. This was quite a sacrifice on the part of my mother. Her biggest encounter with nature was when she walked from our house to the clothesline; now she was going to the wilds of Maine, to a rented cabin without electricity or plumbing.

I remember the drive up, and upon arriving at Greenville, Maine, at the southern end of Moosehead, we still had many miles to drive on a dirt road through spruce and fir forest. Mom didn't say much, probably wondering why on earth she had let us talk her into this. The cabin stood on the shore of this massive lake, nestled under a towering white pine. Right away we all noticed something odd about the cabin. Its little "kitchen" area was in a separate structure, and by structure I mean hut with no electricity but a tiny gas stove, kitchen sink where you used a pump to get water, and cupboards. My mother said, "Now why didn't they put this cooking place inside the cabin?" And I made the mistake of saying, "Maybe to keep the bears away from where we'll be sleeping." Mom's face drained of color, and my dad gave me a severe look and said, "No, it's to keep the mice out." (Years later I heard Dad tell one of his buddies, "You should have seen this cabin. Jerri had to *walk outside* to a hut to cook the food! They had the kitchen separate to keep the bears away from us!")

The cabin was rustic but exactly the kind of mountain or lakeside retreat I dreamed of living in, and of course I mentioned that to my father. But he correctly pointed out that driving this far for a weekend retreat would give him time for a cup of coffee by the lake before he had to get back to the bakery. My mother, not wanting to put a damper on our trip, gamely said something to the effect that someday, when I was older and if I worked hard, my dream might come true. Then she added that this was the most remote place in the world, and she had never been so far from civilization.

"Jerri," said my dad, "just pretend we're pioneers."

"Or cavemen," she answered.

—◆—

We also soon realized the fishing was tougher than casting a Mepps to stocked trout in Laurel Pond at the Fishing Derby. The first day at Moosehead, we couldn't take the boat out because waves pounded the rocky shore as if coming from an angry sea. That night the wind howled, and even though it was technically still summer, the temperature plunged and we fired up the woodstove. The sound of waves booming on the shore, rolling the gravel and small stones, coupled with the wind whipping through the big pine made quite a racket, but I loved every minute of it. Bob did too; this was the kind of place we'd read about in our outdoors books.

The next day the lake was still too choppy for us to use the cabin's boat, and I told my parents that I'd take Bob on a short hike instead. They said fine, reminding me to watch out for my younger brother and not to go too far.

As soon as Bob and I were out the door I said, "We got to move fast and cover ground. We didn't come all this way not to see a moose!" And off we went on the trail that meandered along the shore. The path became more and more faint the farther we went, and when it entered a bog I was concerned I'd get us both lost. It was late August, but I remembered how cold the previous night had been, and the thought of spending the night in the woods—with my parents going ballistic with worry—made me stop and suggest we turn back. The notion of bears wandering around and finding us also crossed my mind. While I was explaining this to Bob, he saw something on the other side of the marsh and whispered, "Look over there."

Across the bog was an enormous dark hulk standing about seven feet high. I'd never seen one of these massive creatures before. There were no moose at Pollywog Pond.

We crouched down and watched. The moose had horns, not a massive spread but big enough and probably still growing for the fall mating season. It stood in about six inches of water eating aquatic plants. We were close enough to see its ears twitching, maybe to flick off flies. I'm not sure if the moose had seen us, but it paid us no mind. (Moose are so large, they have little to fear in the forest and are not hyperalert like so many other wild creatures I've encountered. There is no predator in the Maine woods strong enough to take down a healthy adult moose.)

The bull moose did, however, lift its massive head from the water, plants dripping from its mouth, and look in our direction. Maybe it had seen us but viewed us as no more of a nuisance than the flies buzzing around its head.

"Geez," I whispered to Bob, "it's huge. Looks prehistoric."

"Look at the shoulders."

The shoulders were a mass of humped muscle, and if we were standing next to the moose, I doubt my head would reach their top. Then I remembered my camera was dangling on a cord around my neck. It was a cheap camera with no zoom lens, and when I looked through the viewfinder, the trees and brush in front of us blocked much of the view; any photo would be of poor quality.

I had the passing thought that we were close enough. But then the issue of proof entered my head—I needed tangible confirmation that we had seen a moose up close and personal. The "wise" Mike said to the "impulsive" Mike, "You don't need proof; you and Bob have the experience." The "dumb" Mike shot back, "When are you ever going to get this close to a moose again? Don't be a chicken. Get the picture or no one will believe you." This was the same warped logic that had led me to kill the carp caught in the Meadows just so I could go back and get a photo. At that age, seeking praise by others was just as important as the experience itself. So guess which Mike won out?

"Let's get closer," I said. And so we did, trying not to make a sound. Each time the moose had its head down near or in the water, we'd take a step; when it raised its head, we'd freeze. The moose was not standing still for us but continued grazing, and when we reached a clear area, it had its back to us.

We waited a bit, but the perfect photo opportunity didn't come, and I decided to make the bull turn around. At first I considered clapping my hands but decided that would pinpoint our location. And so I went to Plan B: I'd throw a rock, and that way the moose wouldn't know our position.

Of course I probably should have told Bob what I was going to do, but as I remember it, I simply picked up a rock and hurled it at the moose, hoping the splash would make it lift its head and I'd be ready with the camera.

That is not what happened. The rock hit the moose in the rump.

Then all hell broke loose. For a big ungainly creature, this moose sure did move fast. It whipped its head from the water, spray flinging from its snout high into the air. Then it let out a deep snort, wheeled around, and looked directly at us.

I held my breath.

The bull flattened its ears and lowered its head. Instinct told me it was coming for us and I hollered to Bob, "Run for your life!"

And I ran, branches whipping me in the face. I looked over my shoulder; Bob was behind me, and behind Bob was the enraged moose! The beast had already crossed half the bog and was probably about seventy feet behind us, coming on strong.

Somewhere in the back of my head I'm sure I thought, *How am I going to explain to my parents if I return without Bob?*

A root tripped me up and down I went, doing a complete roll. How Bob managed to avoid me was a miracle, and now he was in the lead. Glancing back toward the bog, I could see the moose had reached the spot where I had thrown the rock. Now on solid ground, he appeared bigger than ever, especially its head. I'm sure that if I took the time, I would have seen the hair bristling on its back.

Picture one of the chase scenes in the movie *Jurassic Park* and you have an idea of my terror trying to keep ahead of this half-ton galloping beast. *Holy shit,* I thought, *we're going to die!*

Back on my feet, I raced past Bob. "It's coming for us!"

Then it hit me: Bob had been entrusted to my care on this hike, and now he was going to be trampled and gored by the moose I had to hit with a rock! I hazarded a look over my shoulder.

The moose was gone. How a creature this large could just melt into the woods was a mystery to me, but I could see no sign of it.

Bob slowed down and looked back too, but neither of us stopped running for another hundred feet. When Bob caught his breath, he gasped, "You idiot! Why did you throw the rock?"

"Never mind the rock. Get one thing through your head: Do not tell Mom or Dad, no matter how tempted you may be."

Bob never squealed on me, and for the first time a family vacation did not involve my father and me butting heads. None of us knew that this was the last vacation we'd all take together—that soon the trajectory of our lives would be changed forever.

Chapter Fourteen

By my junior year of high school, I had my driver's license. In hindsight, giving a sixteen-and-a-half-year-old permission to drive a car is much too young—at least it was in my case. My father took me out on driving lessons; he was calm and full of tips, some of which still go through my head today as I drive. "Don't follow behind a truck, you can't see what's down the road" was one. Another was "Bad things happen when you go fast."

With those two tips, I batted 50 percent, and of course the one I ignored was my driving speed.

One night after working at the supermarket, Dale and I raced each other home, using our parents' cars of course. I drove our monstrous station wagon with the fake wood paneling on the side, and Dale kept up in his family's Rambler. It's a miracle neither Dale nor I crashed or hurt another driver. The only trouble I had was *after* the race, when I entered my street, Ridge Road, and headed home. I was still traveling much too fast, and when I hit the brakes while approaching our driveway, the car went into a sideways skid, coming to rest far up the Goldbergs' lawn near their front door.

Terrified that my parents might have heard the skid and would look out the front door, I slammed the car into reverse and stepped on the accelerator. The technique worked—I shot off the lawn back into the street, but not before chewing up big patches of turf.

The next morning I saw my handiwork and felt awful. Tire marks stretched down the middle of the Goldbergs' lawn, from the street almost to their front door. Their nice green lawn now had brown earthen grooves through its center. I never told anyone, nor did my parents suspect me. My father, upon seeing the neighbors' yard chewed up, probably said, "Some people are real animals. The problem in this country is nothing ever happens to them. A slap on the wrist is all they get and they're back to doing the same thing." I think he said that, because he used those same three sentences almost every night when he watched the news on TV. And now I felt like crap, knowing I was one of those people.

Twice I did serious damage to the car, the worst when I dropped a girl off after a date and went peeling out of her driveway. It was winter, and with snow on the asphalt, I must have veered off the driveway a bit because I heard a terrible screeching sound. I later found out there were granite posts lining the driveway, and our family station wagon "happened" to scrape up against one, which opened the side of the car like a can opener. The fault, I quickly convinced myself, was not my driving but the granite post. How dare those homeowners place such a hazard so close to the driveway. I wondered if my father would see it the same way.

The station wagon was the car my mother used, and for maybe a second I thought I could pin the damage on her. But I wasn't that much of a jerk. Instead, the next day I waited for my father to come home and told him I had put a "scrape" in mom's car. Then I showed it to him. The side of the car looked like I imagine the *Titanic* did after scraping the iceberg—the tear started at the driver's door and extended all the way aft to the stern. Keeping with the *Titanic* analogy, had the car been in the water, the damage would have flooded every ballast chamber, breached several bulkheads, and sunk.

My father shocked me by simply saying I needed to drive slower and that the damage was bad but he'd take care of it. That was it. No hollering, no threats, no nothing.

At the time I had no idea why his response gave me the benefit of the doubt. But now I think I know why: college. He knew my grades were improving each year, and he recognized that I was holding down part-time jobs throughout the year. Putting his kids through college meant everything to him. He never had the chance, and Dad would frequently tell us that a college education opened doors and without it we'd have far fewer options. Slowly, I was coming to think the same thing.

Lynn seemed to be thriving at her university, and when she came home for a visit every couple months, I noticed a new confidence about her, and she seemed happier than ever. When she was home, at her old place at our kitchen table, my dad would be beaming as she described some of her classes and activities. Then Dad would ask her to do an impersonation of one of our neighbors or a movie star; he'd laugh his loud cackle, and my mother would do her "silent" laugh, where her body would shake but barely a peep would come out of her mouth.

Then the conversation would turn back to college, and my dad would comment on how we kids would be among the first generation of his family to go to college, and how he was proud that we boys were doing well at school.

And so I think that's why he was easy on me when I ruined the car. He was changing. Now it was my turn.

I didn't exactly rise to the challenge. While I slowed my driving speed, I simply employed friends for some of my harebrained schemes that involved cars, one of which involved Opie. I had the bright idea that I'd tie a rope to his car's bumper and skateboard behind his car to Booge's house. We started off slow, and I kept giving Opie the thumbs-up to increase his speed, which he did with enthusiasm. We were really moving down one of the main streets in town, Williams Street, and it was all I could do to hang on. I didn't dare take one of my hands off the rope to motion for him to slow down, because I felt I'd fall to the pavement. By the time we got to Laurel Street, I was terrified.

Then came flashing lights and the sound of a siren. Opie didn't pull over right away, and I prayed the cop would somehow make him stop—heck, shoot out his tires if he had to. Finally Opie rolled to a halt, but my momentum kept me zipping along well past his car. When I finally hopped off the skateboard, I walked back to the officer. He told me I was a fool, he told me I was an idiot, and he told me I was damn lucky to be in one piece. I agreed wholeheartedly. That cop might have saved my life.

The police officer took down our names, addresses, and phone numbers. A few kids had gathered on the sidewalk, probably hoping we'd be put in handcuffs and placed in the cruiser. Instead the cop had calmed down and said we were free to go. I guessed he'd be calling my parents, so that night I told both of them what happened. My mother said I was grounded and that I lacked common sense. Strangely, I don't remember my father saying anything, just shaking his head sadly. He might have been thinking, *I got blessed with four children, but one of them is a moron.*

I *was* a moron, but not for the reason they said. There was no need for me to explain about the skateboard incident: The cop never called.

Senior year was a good year. I had a girlfriend I was in love with and a pack of friends that were tight. I gave up on soccer and coaches who were humorless and let kids rot on the bench. Instead I turned my attention back to the outdoors. My buddies and I were all interested in trout fishing, and with our cars we could travel to a sportsman's club we joined and to a little cabin that Cogs's family owned at the edge of the Berkshires. While we didn't have fly rods, we were tying a few flies and casting them with a spinning rod and a casting bubble.

That year was the first year I didn't have detention, but I was still an instigator, hatching new plans for fun. Toward the end of senior year I helped organize "Senior Skip Day," where the entire class was encouraged to go to Misquamicut State Beach on the Rhode Island shore instead of school. I put a couple signs up in the school hallway, told everyone I knew where and when we were going, and the trip was a resounding success. But when I returned to school the next day, the fun was over. Called to the principal's office, I was accused of being the lead instigator. Of course I denied it, but the principal brought out Exhibit A. It was one of the signs I had put up in the hallway, and while it didn't have my name on it, I thought I had better fess up that I was one of several organizers. The principal didn't believe me and was taking an extreme stand, talking about detention for the rest of the year and possibly expulsion. He sent me home from school early that day with a sealed envelope to my parents.

I gave the note to my mother and watched her face get red. This quiet, reserved woman who never made waves staggered me when she blurted out: "How dare they! You're in the National Honor Society, and they think they're going to treat you like a criminal for going to the beach."

I thought she was going to scream at me or break down crying. I'd seen my mother flustered and angry before, but it had been directed at me. Now she was adamantly defending me. And she wasn't done.

"I'm going to the school right now and talk to that principal."

I didn't know what to say. In fact I couldn't speak; I was on the verge of tears. I'd never been so proud of my mother in my life. She was doing something that I thought she was incapable of; this polite and shy five-foot-two lady was going to take on authority.

She did not take me with her to the school, and she was gone for a long time. I was waiting in the kitchen when she came back to the house, and I searched her face to see if she had been crying. She looked exhausted but not beaten.

All she said was "They are not going to expel you, and you don't have detention for the rest of the year. You ended up with a week's detention." I asked a question, but she waved me off and started preparing dinner. She never scolded me, never questioned my common sense, and never brought up the incident again. Best of all, I don't believe she ever told my father.

It was my mother's finest hour. And I'm grateful to her to this day.

We think we know our parents, but they have sides to them that we are often blind to. I'm glad I got a glimpse into the inner resolve my mom showed by rising above her normal tendency to go with the flow and instead challenge someone in power.

<hr />

Choosing a college was where I could have used a mentor or a guidance counselor. After the last uncomfortable exchange with my guidance counselor, that was out of the question, so I made the mistake of following the herd rather than considering the entire college experience and my particular interests. I ultimately decided on Boston College for two main reasons: A couple girls I knew were going there, and it would be close to the university where my girlfriend was going. But right before leaving for BC, the college sent me a letter explaining that because they had an "over-enrollment," not all incoming freshman could live in the campus dorms. Through a lottery, some of us (me) would have to live off campus in apartments. They tried to soften the blow by saying my roommates would be other BC freshmen and that periodic bus service would be provided to and from campus.

So when my dad drove me and my bags to a narrow street in Brighton crowded with apartments, it sure didn't feel like the college setting I was hoping for. Adding to my discomfort was that this was the first time I'd be living in a city atmosphere, with honking cars and police sirens echoing off the brick, concrete, and pavement. I stepped out of the car and took it all in. The buildings blocked out the sun, I saw just one scraggly tree, and the smell of the city was a far cry from Lake Morey, the Pollywog Pond, and the Meadows. A sinking feeling came over me; the place felt more like prison than my new home.

But my dad was upbeat. He was still proud that I had been accepted at Boston College, and he had high hopes for me. He said I'd be a natural for business with the way I handled the various part-time jobs and was able to save some money. Shaking my hand goodbye, he asked me to call and tell him about the one elective course I was taking in history.

There was a bad omen of things to come during that very first month at BC. Opie and Griff had come from their colleges to visit, and while we were walking through campus one night, one of them exchanged words with a BC football player. We kept walking, but the football player hollered something. I looked toward him through the gloom, and a full bottle of beer came flying through the air, smashing into my chin. Blood spurted everywhere, but in the end I got off easy: stitches and what I thought was a concussion. I shudder to think of the damage had I been hit in the eye or temple.

I grew to loathe traveling to campus via bus; there was never any time to go back to my room. Once I was on campus I stayed there, spending hours between classes in the library. And instead of walking to the cafeteria with buddies from a dorm, I'd wander in there alone, not knowing anyone, usually eating by myself. There are few things worse than being young and sitting by yourself gulping down food when everyone around you is with their friends. I felt like I had gone from a popular kid to an outcast overnight.

I made matters worse by rarely staying at BC or with my apartment roommates on the weekends. Instead I'd hitchhike out to a suburb to see my girlfriend. The drivers who stopped were not the Mr. Bargers of the world, who picked up Opie and me on our trip to Maine. I had a number of weirdos stop and offer me rides, one of whom kept a pistol in his free hand while his other was on the steering wheel. And usually, because I was traveling on Route 9, which is mostly local traffic, it would take three or four rides to reach my destination.

Like so many kids who go off to college, my girlfriend met someone new. Through the fall there had been plenty of clues—fewer phone calls, dwindling letters, and less enthusiasm about getting together. Instead of seeing what was right in front of me, I chose to stick my head in the sand and pretend the relationship was fine. She tried her best not to hurt me, but by her doing so, it was a long, incremental breakup. When she finally told me she was in love with someone else, I was devastated. And even worse, I couldn't get mad. She had done nothing wrong and had done her best to let me down easy. Anger would have served me well, but I knew she wasn't to blame.

I'm sure many students have had bad experiences their freshman year, and there's a word for the emotion that most struggle with: loneliness. I had always enjoyed time alone, but in this situation I went for days without any meaningful conversation. What a difference loneliness is from simply being alone. My nights were fitful and sleep was elusive. By December, my goal was simply to get through final exams and go home. Luckily, before the depression hit I had built up all As and one B in my various courses, but after my final exams, which were all Cs or Ds, my final grades were all Bs.

After the Christmas break I went back to BC, but the depression I was suffering from simply would not allow me to focus in class or on my studies. I was thin to begin with, and now I'd lost my appetite; pounds I could not afford to lose seemed to be evaporating, taking my optimism along with them. It was clear to me that I needed a break and felt anxious to leave college behind me. But how would I tell my father?

While he knew I was hurting, I think he was surprised when I called my mother one morning and said something to the effect that I was done, that I couldn't take it anymore. She asked if I was sure and if maybe I needed to give it more time. But I answered I was 100 percent positive and that I was having trouble comprehending the simplest of instructions. I'm sure she heard the desperation in my voice and said she'd talk to my dad and call me back as soon as possible.

The phone rang less than an hour later. "Your father will pick you up right after he gets out of work." That meant that after getting up at 4:00 a.m., he would have to drive to Boston at 4:00 p.m. and then return. I hated to put him through that grind and thought how disappointed he'd be in me and what I might say on the long car ride home.

I will never forget that two-hour drive with my Dad on the Mass Pike in the dark, heading back to Longmeadow. For the first time it felt like it was just the two of us, and we were talking—no shouting, no being a wise guy, no trying to explain things from my point of view. Knowing I was despondent, he showed nothing but love in his words and actions. He didn't second-guess my decision; he didn't bring up the money he'd lose paying for the semester and didn't pepper me with questions. Instead, he talked about the disappointments in his own teenage years, from being jilted by a girlfriend to having the police bring him home to face his father after some discrepancy. I'd never heard these stories before, and I just mumbled a few comments, letting him do most of the talking. Perhaps he thought I was too depressed to process what he was saying, but his message came through loud and clear: He not only cared but he loved me and was trying his best to understand me. Fathers back in 1973 didn't say those things out loud, and he didn't, but I knew.

CHAPTER FIFTEEN

ONCE BACK HOME, I SLOWLY FOUND MY WAY OUT OF THE BLACK HOLE. Work was a big help. I labored at the bakery with my dad a couple days a week; the other days I worked at the supermarket. This was a good mix, as it forced me to be around lots of different people and engage in the world again. My laughter, however, was gone, and while I was productive, I felt robotic, as though I was going through the motions of living but the joy was absent. When you're eighteen years old, it's hard to see you have a whole life ahead of you.

My mom suggested I go to a therapist, and I think she was surprised that I readily agreed. I was determined to get my life back, but I just didn't know how to do it on my own. My therapist was wonderful, basically pointing out that shit happens, people change, and up until my bad college experience and getting dumped by my girlfriend, things had come fairly easy to me. He also taught me not to pretend there wasn't a problem when it was staring me right in the face, referring to all the clues my girlfriend had been dropping before the breakup. He said something like "Ignoring the problem won't make it go away; you got to talk about it to whoever is involved."

I was also learning my own resilience skills, and that included letting time pass. It was folly to think I'd just wake up one day, the pain would be gone, and I'd be my old self. But as big chunks of time went by, things slowly got better, and my mantra became "Let time pass." Another technique I learned was to keep busy, to force myself to go through the motions of being social, working with the right attitude, and, most importantly, do something productive. I saved some money from the bakery work, and gave it back to my father for the down payment on the second semester at BC he lost. He told me to keep the money, that I'd need to buy a car soon. But when he saw how serious I was, he realized this was part of my healing and accepted the payment. (When it did come time to buy a car, that money was handed back to me.)

Reading was one activity that helped time pass and let the scars heal. I read many of the history books in my father's collection, some of my mother's spiritual books, and renewed my habit of riding my bike to the library and loading up my backpack with adventure books and novels. One of my favorites at the time was *Bright Flows the River* by Taylor Caldwell. Books have the power to help you through tough times by taking you out of yourself and transporting you to another world or another time.

In high school we read Thoreau's *Walden*, and now I picked it up again. Parts of the book still seemed too slow and dense to hold my attention, but every now and then I'd come across a nugget of wisdom. One passage I underlined was "I learned this, at least, by my experiment: that if one advances confidently in the directions of his dreams, and endeavors to live the life which he has imagined, he will meet with a success unexpected in common hours."

I wasn't sure what my big dream was, but my small dream was just to feel like my old self again. The long-range vision of owning my cabin seemed to be extinguished by thoughts of what I was going to do in the fall: go back to college or investigate better-paying jobs. At least I didn't have the threat of Vietnam hanging over me. Although I had registered for the draft several months back, the US involvement in the war officially ended in 1973, and curtailment of the draft soon followed. Nixon referred to the Paris Peace Accords that terminated our fighting in Vietnam as "Peace with Honor," but in reality we threw the South Vietnamese under the bus.

I also read Norman Vincent Peale's *The Power of Positive Thinking*, and his message seemed to be in line with Thoreau's, with the main difference being that Peale's book was rooted in Christianity and faith. I was never religious in the way my mother was, and had long since stopped going to the Catholic church, but I did believe in God. However, my belief system was evolving, and while I figured prayer to a higher power could give me strength, I didn't buy into the idea that God had any involvement here on earth. I figured he was hands-off, that miracles were luck, and that there was a randomness to life.

While I can't say that I'm glad I went through those tough months, I found it true that adversity gives people new insights, wisdom, and toughness. But most importantly for me, however, was that the experience led me to have deeper empathy for others and do a better job at reaching out to them. And that included my father.

We didn't have the conversations I craved, but I began to understand why we didn't talk like the night he drove me home from BC. On our ride to the bakery at 4:30 a.m., we were still waking up, and on the way home we were too tired. Beyond that we simply weren't around each other that much, which was a good thing, because it meant I was out of the house making new friends. My dad also never put pressure on me to go back to school, move out of the house, or find a job other than the bakery. I'm not sure if he liked having me at the bakery or if his life would have been simpler had he managed the place without his son underfoot.

My dad had a smile on his face when he saw me filling out college applications at the kitchen table, and the smile got bigger when I was accepted and decided to attend Saint Michael's College in Vermont. This time I gave more thought to what college to attend than I had before. Saint Mike's seemed a good fit for me because it was in a state I loved, close to the mountains and lakes that held a spell over me as a kid, and I had two friends who went there, so I was able to stay with them at the school, getting a feel for the place. I was even able to talk my high school buddy Dale into going there, and we would be roommates.

At Saint Mike's I was determined not to make the mistake I made at BC by not seeking out new friends. That led me to say yes to anything and everything, and most of what I did my first year there, I did to excess. I was back to my old self, pushing boundaries and seeking to make up for lost time by chasing women, consuming beer, and smoking weed way more than was healthy.

The little city of Burlington, Vermont, not far from campus, was like the Wild West, with fights and drunkenness a regular feature on weekends, and I spent far too much time at places like the Last Chance Saloon. But somehow at Saint Mike's I also managed to juggle studies, play, and work, taking six courses instead of the usual five to make up for the semester I missed while holding down a part-time job at the school cafeteria. And instead of soccer or wrestling, I was playing touch football and volleyball and having a ball.

Pushing myself to the limit, I soon contracted mononucleosis, and for the first part of the spring semester I was forced to slow down. While I did recover, I found my tolerance for alcohol much lower than before the illness, and hangovers were severe. That, of course, was another lesson learned the hard way, but it was probably a blessing. Now, instead of going to bars in Burlington both Friday and Saturday nights, the illness forced me to spend one of those nights getting rest in my room. Dorm mates looked at me like I had lost my mind when I'd come back from the library late on a Saturday afternoon loaded down with books for pleasure reading. They were already intoxicated from "pregaming" before their night out, and they couldn't understand why I'd voluntarily stay in.

One of the authors I discovered at the college library was Ray Stannard Baker, who sometimes used the pen name David Grayson. While Baker had written many nonfiction works of biography and history, along with dozens of articles on the theme of muckraking, he somehow found the time to write semiautobiographical books about his years living at his farm in Amherst, Massachusetts. Those were the books I consumed during the spring of 1975, and they rekindled my desire to spend more time in the woods. He, like me, had had a bad experience living in a city and was overambitious:

> *My senses, my nerves, even my muscles were continually strained to the utmost of attainment. For many years I never rested. I neither thought nor reflected, I had no pleasure even though I pursued it fiercely during the brief respite of vacations. All these things happened in cities and among crowds. I like to forget them. One day—it was April and the soft maples in the city park were just beginning to blossom—I stopped suddenly. Until I stopped I did not know the pace I ran. It came to me with indescribable poignancy, the thought of walking barefoot in cool, fresh plow furrows as I had done when I was a boy.*

It seemed those lines were directed squarely at me. Yes, I had escaped the city and found a better fit in Vermont, but was I taking advantage of it? Was I rushing along and not realizing the pace I ran? The answer was clear: I was spending too much time in bars and indoors in general, and I'd been chasing my own tail with daily schedules that were packed to the brim with study, work, and then hard-charging play. Grayson's words about walking in fresh plow furrows made me think of the Meadows and all those natural places that brought me both adventure and contentment. And contentment was what Baker/Grayson stressed:

> *Is it not marvelous how far afield some of us are willing to travel in pursuit of that beauty which we leave behind us at home? We mistake unfamiliarity with beauty.*

And here I had the whole state of Vermont in my backyard! And I had the means to explore it with a beat-up Datsun I had bought with my bakery and supermarket earnings. After reading two or three of his books, I vowed to spend some of my time in the woods rather than bars. Friends and I started fishing, and besides trout we caught giant northern pike near where the Lamoille River flows into Lake Champlain. We hiked up rivers with backpacks stuffed with cheap sleeping bags and a tent and camped at waterfalls such as the one at Jeffersonville. And I looked forward to the late spring, when I'd brave the frigid waters we fished in to go swimming and snorkeling. That spring, water was a central part of my life, the way it had been before college.

My free time now had an adventure theme that did not always involve alcohol but instead was connected with the woods and water. That was clearly a good trade-off, because I still had some aftereffects from my mononucleosis. But it also led me to near disaster.

We should have known better. Riding a thirty-dollar raft down an angry river during spring snowmelt is never a good idea. And it was my idea.

That spring I convinced a friend from my dorm to join me for a short raft ride down the Huntington River. I was itching to try out the tiny raft I had bought from the now-defunct discount department store chain, Bradlees. And being impatient and impulsive, I didn't want to wait for lower water levels—I intended to go now, and Rob was game to give it a try. An added impetus was that the Winooski River Raft Race was scheduled to be held in a few days, and we considered this a practice run.

Driving my Datsun B-210 south from Saint Michael's College, we followed Route 2 along the Winooski River. Initially I thought we'd do a short run on this large waterway that originates in the mountains above Montpelier before making a northwest turn, heading for Lake Champlain. The river, however, was a chocolate-colored mess surging over its banks as if a dam had broken. Too much rain on top of a snowpack can do that.

We needed a Plan B, and after looking at my map we decided to check out the Huntington River, a tributary of the Winooski. During the prior summer I'd swum in the large pools of the Huntington River at an area known as The Gorge and learned it could be treacherous. Locals called it "Killer Gorge" or "The Black Hole." The Gorge had claimed several lives, and continues to do so to this day. Unsuspecting swimmers either get sucked into a vortex formed by the narrow flume carved through granite, or the deceptively fast current whisks them from a pool and sends them over the falls, where they get trapped by submerged debris. The Gorge is especially dangerous in late spring or when water is high and the caverns are underwater.

The ominous name Killer Gorge should have deterred us from going anywhere near this river in the spring, but I figured we'd be safe putting in below the gorge itself. And so I drove the Datsun up the dirt road along the river, heading deeper into the mountains. I literally pushed the gas pedal all the way to the floorboard, because that piece-of-junk car had absolutely no power, and on steep hills I worried that it would come to a stop. Looking back, I wish it had.

After several minutes of driving we reached the gorge and then did a U-turn and parked well below the narrow twisting walls of the chasm and its waterfalls. Rob and I carried our raft down through the woods toward the river, trudging through muck and snow. In some spots there was a foot of snow under the hemlocks. The woods were gloomy and dank, unique to early spring, when the forest floor is saturated. The snow was discolored and crumbling, and the trees were bare under overcast skies.

We were dressed in sneakers, blue jeans, and windbreakers. In our free hands—thank God—were life jackets along with our paddles.

Reaching the river, we found that the spring runoff had swollen it to such proportions that water overflowed the banks and raced around the trunks of trees. And in the river proper there was plenty of whitewater in the boulder-strewn channel, which was normally quite shallow. Rather than concentrating on these alarming signs, I focused on the river's color. The Huntington was nowhere near as dirty-brown as the Winooski, and I took this as a good sign.

"What do you think?" asked Rob.

"I say we go for it. If we find it's too powerful, we'll just paddle to the side and get out."

And so we agreed to give it a go, without giving a thought to first scouting the river below us. We assumed riding the river would be no different than riding in my Datsun; we could just pull over when we needed to. The river had other ideas. From the moment we launched, it was in control and not us.

Rob, being the stronger one, took the back position in the yellow raft, and I took the front. I was supposed to bark out directions around boulders, but that was a joke—instead we just tried to position the raft in the deepest part of the river to avoid careening directly into rocks or downed trees close to the banks. But more than once, we received glancing blows from boulders. Icy splashes of water came in over the bow, but we barely noticed. We were having fun, playing on the edge.

The speed at which we were carried was a thing to behold, and more than once we whooped and hollered from a mix of joy, adrenaline, and fear. Every drop of water in that river was finding the path of least resistance, and the Huntington felt like a living creature fleeing from the mountain.

—✦—

Considering the raft was more of a kid's toy than a sturdy vessel, it held up quite well, and none of the rocks tore its inflated rubber bottom. I was thinking how lucky we were, how exciting the thrill, and how good it would be to climb out of the raft onto the ground and say we did it. In those first two or three minutes of the exhilarating ride we mistakenly thought we had some control over the surging river because we managed to stay in its middle. But we soon learned that was pure luck—or simply the river toying with us.

─ ⌣ ─

When we first launched the raft, we were sitting on the bottom of its floor, but we realized that to have any leverage with our paddles, we needed to be in a kneeling position. And so we were up on our knees, digging into the water with our paddles as quickly as possible. It's a wonder the raft didn't swing around sideways or even turn 180 degrees, but we managed to keep the bow in the front. More than once I glanced down at the knot I'd tied with my life jacket straps to make sure it was secure. I wanted to make the bulky orange life jacket tighter, but I didn't dare stop paddling.

The feeling of being swept along might be akin to an inexperienced horseback rider whose mount got spooked by a bear or rattlesnake, causing it to bolt, the rider hanging on for fear of being thrown. That was certainly my mindset as I began to realize who was in control. *Just ride this out, and at the first pool paddle for shore.*

This section of river, however, had no deep pools but rather was one continuous rapid, and it hurled us along like so much flotsam. (Thoreau described the experience as "navigating a thunder spout" when he was paddling on Webster Stream in Maine.) Several times we bounced off or over submerged boulders marked by frothing water forced to either side of the obstruction. At the downstream side of small ledges, the water looked especially angry where it curled back on itself in frustrated confusion, and I held my breath until we were by these seething spots. *So far, so good,* I thought; *now let's get to shore.*

─ ⌣ ─

We could hear the waterfall before we could see it. Crashing turbulence was somewhere up ahead, but falling water is difficult to spot when you are coming downstream to it.

"Pull over! Left, left!" I shouted.

Our frenzied paddling had absolutely no effect on our course. A sickening wave of panic shot through me, and I thought I was going to puke.

Perhaps a second, maybe two, went by. Then there was just air under the front of the raft where I was kneeling. The drop was no more than four feet, but the water surged over the edge with a terrifying roar and took us with it.

During the drop I was ejected into the river, and then the raft, with Rob still in it, plowed into me, driving me under. Every neuron in my body screamed *up, up, up.* I flailed, kicked, and twisted, so terrified of not surfacing, I never registered just how cold the water was. But the river held me underwater, as if to say, *You fool, you thought this was a game.*

Two or three seconds after tumbling, I popped up next to the raft and grabbed hold of it. Something similar must have happened to Rob, because he too emerged from the icy water and grabbed hold of the raft. The whirlpool of water below the drop kept Rob and me together along with the raft, but now we had to get out of its clutches.

For a second or two the swirling current spun the raft around and around, trapped downstream of the boulders we'd gone over. My chest felt tight, and my breath came in little gasps as we twirled. *We're not getting out of this; we are going to die right here.*

Then the whirlpool suddenly spit us out, and the river pushed us hard into some rocks, where the raft briefly got hung up. I tried to climb inside the raft, but my legs were lead weights dragging behind my body.

My next thought was an odd one, but I have to be honest. I remember thinking, *I don't want to die alone. I'm glad Rob is here.* It was a terrible, selfish frame of mind. I wish I could say I wanted Rob there so he could live and tell my parents what happened to me, but the truth was I just didn't want to die alone.

The first words spoken since we went overboard were Rob's, and they were the exact opposite of what I wanted to hear.

"I'm going numb! I'm going to let go and try to swim!"

"Noooo!" I shouted. "Just hang on!"

Too late. Rob released his hold on the raft, and the current snatched him. For a second or two I watched him bob downstream, then he disappeared. It was awful.

I too was getting numb from the cold, and as water cascaded around my shoulders, I decided to push off from the rocks. But there was no way I was letting go of the raft. I was convinced it was my only means of salvation. Using my feet I shoved off from a boulder; the raft and I were free of the whirlpool and were whisked downstream.

Several times my legs hit rocks or my feet scraped the river bottom, but the sheer volume of moving water made it impossible to stand or angle toward the shore. Once I used one arm to reach out and grip a jagged rock in slower water, but the charging river yanked me off. I could feel my strength ebbing.

At a bend in the river, the current swept me close to shore; I reached for overhanging branches but could not get a grip. Nor could I get a grip on my emotions: Frustration and fear were overtaking resolve and fortitude, and tears were mixing with the icy water.

Then as suddenly as the river's flow raced us over the falls, it deposited me in an eddy, and I could stand in waist-deep water. I hauled myself and the raft out of the water and onto the snow-covered bank. For a second I caught my breath, sitting on the edge of the raft, but then I thought of Rob and a feeling of dread, colder than any river, spread through me. *Where is he? I brought him to this river . . .*

I started walking down the riverbank, sloshing through water, mud, and snow, calling out for Rob. After a hundred yards I was in full panic, running and screaming his name.

Then I saw him. He was still in the Huntington. Rob had found a snagged branch in the river that allowed him to hold position approximately twelve feet from the bank. His head and shoulders were out of the rushing river, but the rest of his body was being pummeled. The torrent surrounded him, and there was no slack water in sight.

Hollering for him to hang on another minute—as if he had a choice—I frantically searched for something that would reach him. A small dead tree was the best I could do, but when I tried to extend it to him, I realized the tree was a bit short; the current swept it back to shore.

Rob shouted for me to do it again. This time, when the tip of the fallen tree was closest to him, he lunged for it and caught the end with one hand and then got a firm grip with the other. All I had to do was hang on to my end and the surging river did the rest, swinging him and the tree to shore.

I don't recall any celebration, just relief. It was a long slog back to my car, and once inside we took off our clothes, blasted the heater, and headed back to school, having survived our own stupidity.

———

A week or two later, Rob and I watched the Great Winooski Raft Race from the safety of shore. The participants fared little better than we did. Most entries were homemade rafts, some using metal drums that might have been empty beer kegs for floats. Colorful flags and banners streamed from the vessels, and one crew used snow shovels instead of paddles, adding to the event's festive air. The rafts were in all shapes and sizes, and many were crammed with five or six passengers, hooting and hollering, likely fueled by alcohol. They went flying down the churning brown river and performed surprisingly well—until they reached the railroad bridge.

As I had learned, steering a raft in swift-moving water is no easy task, and more than one of the vessels slammed into the railroad bridge's cement pilings. The homemade rafts either crumbled into two or three pieces or were forced high up on the pilings, and riders went tumbling off in different directions. Some of those flailing in the frigid water made it to shore and some were rescued by other rafters, but I remember seeing two people clinging to the bridge abutments, too terrified to hop into the angry river and swim for shore.

Oddly, most spectators didn't seem to realize the peril the stranded rafters were in—but I knew. I knew the fear, the risk of hypothermia, and the possibility of drowning if they tried to swim for it. Police and firefighters were called to the scene, and those trapped on the abutment eventually were rescued. Those same first responders, as well as college officials, later made sure that 1975 was the last river race run. But I didn't know that at the time, and I couldn't help but think about designing a raft out of Styrofoam and entering the race the following year. It was as if my life-and-death incident on the Huntington River had happened to someone else—my zest for adventure overruled common sense.

CHAPTER SIXTEEN

THAT SUMMER I FOUND A JOB THAT PAID SLIGHTLY MORE THAN THE bakery and the supermarket: I became a janitor at an elementary school. Most of the classrooms were empty, but there were two summer classes in session at the far wing of the school. The job was incredibly boring and a bit lonely. There was a lead janitor and his assistant who worked at the school full-time, and I was the rookie hired for the summer to help perform a complete cleaning of the school.

I found myself in empty classrooms, scrubbing floors and removing gum from desks; if I was lucky, I was allowed to use the giant floor polisher, which I could barely control. Rather than me guiding the machine, it pulled me down the darkened hallways much the same way the Huntington River had swept me downstream.

The outdoor work was equally isolating, including cutting the lawn, trimming the bushes, and weeding around the school's foundation.

In midsummer I considered quitting and going back to the supermarket just to be around more people, but I put a halt to that idea when the lead janitor told me to go outside and wash all the windows. Making my way down the back of the school, I came to the two classrooms that were occupied. As I washed the windows of the first classroom, I looked inside and saw an attractive young teacher standing in front of the class. I waved at her, and she smiled back.

The next day I decided that I had done a poor job on the windows of that classroom and went back with my little ladder and cleaned them again. The teacher was sitting with a group of students, but she did give me a smile as my squeegee squeaked along the already-spotless windows. I was back again the next day, ready to pull every weed along the foundation near her classroom. Just as I got started, the teacher led the entire class outside and assembled them under the shade of an oak tree. Maybe she decided story time would be better in the fresh air.

I couldn't just barge into the middle of her session, but I found enough microscopic weeds to keep on pulling and stay near the group. When she herded the kids inside, I finally had my chance to speak to her. I asked what she did at lunchtime, and she said she usually ate in the classroom. I suggested we have lunch under the big oak and she could read to me.

Our lunches soon turned into something more. This young teacher was still living at her parents' house, and conveniently, both of them worked during the day. Even better, the house had a beautiful pool and patio in the backyard. A tall fence gave the pool total privacy, another happy coincidence.

To keep the story PG-13, I won't go into details, other than to say my lunch periods got longer and longer, making the lead janitor furious when I returned floating in a happy haze of love.

Somehow I hung on to the job until the end of the summer, and I went back to Saint Mike's thinking the teacher and I were madly in love.

But here is where the budding writer in me facilitated my demise. I wrote long letters to the teacher, and apparently her mother read one of them, which happened to include my waxing poetic about our trysts at her house.

The mother kicked the teacher out of the house, and the young lady found an apartment—with a pool—where she promptly met a guy her own age and fell in love. Once again I was the jilted boyfriend.

While the breakup hurt, it caused no lasting damage. I'd learned a thing or two about being resilient, and I returned undeterred to my bachelorhood. One of the highlights of that year was a trip my college buddies and I made to Florida. Someone, I believe it was my friend Sully, had the bright idea that we could save money by renting an old Winnebago and driving down. We all jumped at the chance, and apparently Sully wasn't good at saying no to anyone. Fifteen of us jammed inside that Winnebago!

Our troubles started long before we reached Florida, when somewhere just south of New York City on Interstate 95, our motor home started to fall apart, literally. It was nighttime; most of the guys were sleeping in the back, while I was sitting in the passenger seat next to the driver, who I recall was Sully. Both of us noticed the Winnebago was shaking more than normal. Thank God we had the sense to pull over, stop, and check things out. I remember one of us noticed a tire was missing several lug nuts. I reached out to one of the two remaining nuts, and when I touched it, it fell into my hand. We were that close to the catastrophe of having the tire roll off the vehicle.

The police soon arrived, and I explained what happened while they called a tow truck. In the interest of safety, the police ordered everyone out of the Winnebago and told us to wait behind the guardrail. *This should be interesting*, I thought.

The side door opened up, and a cloud of marijuana smoke escaped the vehicle. The cops watched as one student after another stepped down to the pavement. When the ninth or tenth one stumbled out, the police officer next to me asked just how many kids were in there. I innocently replied that there were just a few more left. The cop shook his head.

The tow truck came, and the driver immediately called for additional help. While I can't remember all the details, I do recall they had to temporarily shut down the interstate while they worked on the Winnebago. And perhaps because we were respectful to the police, they never did search the mobile home for pot. Maybe they were afraid to go inside.

When the vehicle was finally fixed, the rest of the drive south went without incident. We passed the time playing cards, and I decided we should have wrestling matches in the back of the Winnebago, where a giant mattress could be pulled down. Friends bet on who would win, and the cheering and jeering were thunderous as the matches ensued.

Sleeping was difficult with all the snoring, farting, and lack of space. I found that with a little bit of bodily contortion, I could fit in a cupboard that was head high and just aft of the driver's cab. Another smaller friend and I took turns sleeping up there.

Once in Florida, we did all the things students do on spring break, but we were smart enough to have a designated driver who did not drink. I think it was my turn when we were at Daytona Beach. I drove the Winnebago onto the beach and parked the vehicle a safe distance from the water. We all went our separate ways looking for girls and then came back to the mobile home for sleep. When I woke up in the morning, I looked out the window and noticed five or six people standing on the sand just staring at our vehicle. I realized why when I stepped out the side door and my foot landed in an inch of water. The tide was coming up!

We were able to extricate ourselves from the soft sand, but I wonder now if that early-morning bunch of people were hoping we'd be carried out to sea. I don't recall any of them pounding on the Winnebago to let us know what was happening.

———

My other lasting memory of that year at Saint Mike's was a practical joke gone bad. It involved my roommate, Dale, who shared a postal box with me at the school mail room (yes, there really were mail rooms at school in pre-internet/smartphone days). One day I opened the mailbox and there was one of Dale's term papers, complete with a note from the professor on the first page that said, "Nice job, much better this time. B+." I knew all about this term paper, because Dale had worked his butt off on it when his first entry did not meet the instructor's high standards. Luckily, Dale persuaded the instructor to allow him to resubmit the paper, but he had to do so in twenty-four hours. Dale researched and wrote well into the night, dropped the second effort at the professor's office, then held his breath to see what grade he would get. He told me that anything below a C would cause him to fail the class.

In my wisdom, I thought this was an opportunity to give Dale a scare without doing permanent harm. I took his term paper back to our room—Dale was at a different class—and retyped page one exactly as Dale had written it. Then in red pen I scribbled these words across the top: "D-. Dale, I'm disappointed in you. This is no better than your first try." Then I signed the teacher's name.

I put the paper back in our mailbox, told the guys on our floor what I'd done, and waited for Dale to return to our room. When he did, I casually said, "There's mail for you in our box, I think it's your big term paper." Dale made a U-turn and headed for the post office.

While he was retrieving his paper, a bunch of us took up positions at the window at the end of the hall, which afforded us a clear view of the building that held the little postal room in its basement. We waited for Dale to come out, and when he did we gasped. The door to the building was kicked open, and Dale emerged with the paper held high above his head. Not addressing anyone in particular, he angrily shouted to the sky, "You can't f—ing win! You just can't f—ing win!"

Then Dale marched back to our dorm, shaking his head, like a bull about to charge.

The guys who were with me scattered like leaves in the wind. I scurried back to our room, telling myself that I'd gone too far—should immediately tell Dale what I had done and apologize. We were the best of friends, but I wasn't sure how he'd react when I let him in on my little joke. I thought about putting on my bike helmet.

I waited and waited, and when he still didn't come to the room, I hazarded a peek down the hall. I could see Dale at the pay phone. This was not a good sign. I grabbed the original page one of his paper with the B+ on it and trotted to Dale.

"What's up Dale?" I asked.

"I'm calling this asshole professor who just gave me an f—ing D, that's what's up!"

I handed him his original first page, made sure he looked at it, and then ran for my life.

I'm not sure how this next part happened, but either by kicking open the door of the building the post office was in or by kicking the wall by the phone, Dale broke his toe. A big dance was scheduled that weekend, and I remember driving Dale and our dates to the event. While I danced up a storm, Dale sat on a chair with his bandaged right foot elevated on another chair, glaring at me.

Dale and I are good friends to this day, which tells you something: He's nuts!

There were plenty more jokes and great parties that fall of 1976. I also continued my habit of carving out time for both the outdoors and pleasure reading. My insomnia never really left me from my days at BC, and I always had a stack of books by my bed for middle-of-the night reading. I even took up my dad's practice of keeping my favorite quotes from authors in a small notebook that I still have today.

This may sound like I was maturing, and I was, but I'd still revert to impulsive moves I'm not particularly proud of. One occurred in the late fall of 1976, when a college club organized a tricycle race. It involved entering a team of four riders who would relay around a makeshift racetrack, making several required pit stops to chug a beer. Being ultracompetitive, I wanted to win this asinine competition, so I assembled a team of guys all my size, five-foot-seven, thinking our short legs would give us an advantage over the fifteen other teams.

Not wanting to buy a tricycle for a single race, we decided to "borrow" one, which we did by grabbing it off a side street without asking permission. We won the race, for which we received a little trophy and a case of beer. Instead of returning the tricycle, we decided we'd drink the beer first. One thing led to another, and the next morning we still had not returned the tricycle.

Our dorm RA (resident assistant) pounded on my door that morning, shouting that the dean of the college wanted to see me pronto. I had a sinking suspicion what he would say. In the dean's office, he pointed at me and barked, "I had a call from a four-year-old's mother . . ."

I tried to beat him to the punch: "I'm bringing that tricycle back immediately; we lost track of time yesterday."

Acting like he didn't hear me, he said, "Do you know I could expel you for this?"

All I could think of was my father. Just when he and I were starting to see eye to eye, I'd have to explain this to him. "Well, Dad, you see the college decided to expel me because I took a four-year-old's bike."

I pleaded with the dean, explaining I'd never done anything like this before, and it was totally out of character for me. I promised the tricycle would be back on the kid's porch in fifteen minutes.

He agreed, with the caveat that I personally apologize to the child and his mother.

I dodged a major bullet, and thought maybe the dean believed me when I said this incident was out of character for me. That night all my past transgressions came flooding back to me: breaking the middle school detention record, being pulled over for skateboarding behind Opie's car, Senior Skip Day, the girl in my sleeping bag, cheating on guessing the beans in the jar, and on and on. Was this just part of my DNA, or did other people my age do the same things and not get caught?

I must have decided on the latter, because I continued seeking excitement, amusement, and adventures—but tried to be a tad more discreet.

CHAPTER SEVENTEEN

THE FUN DAYS OF COLLEGE CAME TO A SCREECHING HALT IN FEBRUARY 1976. That's when I got the phone call. I was in my dorm room when a friend knocked on my door and told me my mom was on the pay phone. I had a bad feeling from the get-go because my parents never called me, knowing I was impossible to reach and that I would call them once a month.

I can still see that pay phone in the hallway of the dorm and remember how I stood there, stock-still, listening to my mother. She told me my sister, Lynn, and her newlywed husband had been in a car accident. She said it was bad. Then there was silence.

Finally I asked how bad, and she said, "Lynn's in a coma."

I could hear my mother softly crying.

I asked where my father was, and she said he was by Lynn's side.

"I better come home," I finally said.

My mother caught her breath, and said yes, but I should finish up my classes for the week and get home on the weekend. She said the most important thing I could do was pray.

And pray I did. When I got to Longmeadow a couple days later, it was unnerving walking into that house on Ridge Road and seeing Mark and Bob so distraught. They told me my parents were at the hospital. They said Lynn's husband had a broken leg and cuts, but Lynn had suffered a brain injury.

Somehow I pieced together what had happened. Just a month earlier I'd been home for Lynn's wedding, and it was a grand time. Lynn and I were not particularly close when I was in high school, but after my BC experience we exchanged letters, and when I saw her, I knew we had turned the page and were growing closer. At her wedding I remember being so happy for her, wondering why it took me so long to see what a special person she was. Lynn was just twenty-three years old, her husband twenty-five or twenty-six.

When Lynn and her husband returned home from their honeymoon, they decided to drive from their apartment in Connecticut to see my parents. After the visit they were driving south on Interstate 91 when a vehicle traveling north veered across the median strip, went airborne, and landed on top of the car Lynn was in. I later learned that the young man driving the other vehicle was drunk, operating without any insurance; he survived with just minor cuts. Back in 1976 the drunk driving laws were so lax that the man was never incarcerated. A friend of my father's told me he got off with just a one-hundred-dollar ticket for reckless driving.

I was anxious about going to the hospital, afraid that if I started to cry I'd never stop. Mark had prepared me as best he could, explaining how Lynn's hair was shaved off, her head bruised and swollen. When I arrived in her room, I felt numb, and not a tear came out. Nor could I speak, my emotions tightly bottled up inside me. If my parents had not been in the room, I'd have wondered if this person with tubes and wires attached to her body was really my sister. I took my cue from my father and held Lynn's hand; I finally found my voice, telling her it was Michael and that I loved her. A rage was welling up inside me over the unfairness of it all, and I left the room quickly before I exploded.

To see her like that hurt to the core—worst of all was the helpless feeling that there wasn't a damn thing I could do about it. A surgeon relieved some of the swelling in Lynn's brain, but the bottom line was that the prognosis was not good. If she survived, she would likely stay in a coma.

She did survive, and if my memory is correct, she opened her eyes after a week or two, but that was all she was able to do. She showed no sign that she recognized any of us or could hear us. Doctors said her left side was paralyzed, and they were uncertain about her right side. My parents and her husband stayed by her side almost around the clock.

After seven weeks in the hospital, Lynn was transferred to a rehabilitation center outside of Boston. It was a dismal, poorly run establishment, made all the more depressing when I saw several young people with shattered bodies: a little girl who fell off a swing and was paralyzed, a seventeen-year-old boy with his leg amputated from a motorcycle crash, and on and on. So many tragedies that the public briefly hears about when an accident happens, but we never learn the long-term story.

I wondered how many of the long-term patients with chronic conditions had frequent visitors. Did loved ones come every day the first few months then dwindle to weekly, monthly, and later only on birthdays and Christmas? I'll bet you find out who your true friends are when you're immobilized and unable to be part of the crowd.

I remember both my mother and father were disgusted with Lynn's treatment at the rehab center, and after a couple weeks they made the decision to take her home. Lynn would require around-the-clock care, but my parents simply had to have her back at home and knew they could do a better job than the facility. When they informed Lynn's doctor of their decision, he said, "You're making a big mistake. You don't know what you're getting into." My father responded that their decision was final, and they had learned how to work the feeding tube, the shunt, and all the other medical devices. But the system was against them, and they had trouble finding a doctor who would sponsor them. My mother spent days on the phone until she finally located a doctor who agreed to come by the house periodically. This doctor also said taking her home would be too much for one couple to handle and that from his review of the medical records, Lynn would never be able to be moved from her bed. But when my mother said leaving her in the rehab center was not an option, he agreed to sponsor her and be her primary doctor.

And so Lynn was brought back to Longmeadow, and a hospital bed was set up in her room. During the day when my father worked, a home health aide assisted my mother. At night both my parents provided her care. I'm not sure if my father got more than two or three hours of sleep at night. On weekends Lynn's husband cared for her, making the long drive from his job in Connecticut to Longmeadow. I can only imagine how heartbreaking it must have been for him, but he never complained and he showered Lynn with love. Mark was in college in Massachusetts and returned to Longmeadow every weekend to help around the house and with Lynn. Bob was in high school and living at home, so he spent time daily with my sister. All of them talked to Lynn with messages of love and encouragement, hoping she processed what they said.

Back at school my mind was always on Lynn, and I felt fragile. For the longest time I couldn't even say her name for fear of crying. When friends asked how she was doing, I'd give a two-word answer: "the same." One friend, who probably meant well, would ask me about my sister on a daily basis, as if she had a cold and would be well in no time. He never seemed to understand that the mere mention of her name caused me pain, and that my rote answer of "the same" meant that I didn't want to talk about it. But the only thing worse than that annoying friend were the people who didn't say anything at all. If you're ever in doubt in a situation like that, just say something like "You and your sister are in my thoughts." The person you say it to will let you know if they want to discuss it further. Saying the wrong thing is better than saying nothing at all.

One conversation I had in my head over and over was "Why Lynn?" *I* was the reckless one in the family—from slamming a hole on thin ice at Pollywog Pond when I was twelve or thirteen to the more-recent raft ride down the Huntington River. I also wondered if I had had some kind of premonition about her accident, because just a week before it happened I had picked a book from a pile I had brought to college to read; it was my sister's copy of *Death Be Not Proud*. Another thought was one of revenge: I wanted to harm the driver who had done this to her. And finally there was worry: With no insurance money, how would my parents be able to afford a home health aide, and what kind of toll would the nonstop care given by my mother, father, and Lynn's husband extract from them? Would their own health suffer as a consequence? All these thoughts stewed in my head, and stayed there. I should have sought counseling but never did.

When a young person suffers a severe brain injury, it is especially tough because there is no closure, no finite ending as there is in death. The old Lynn was gone, but of course there was no funeral, no communal mourning. Her injury kept me off balance: There were moments of hope when she made the smallest improvement, followed by longer periods of despair when she regressed or ran a fever. The way I coped was to accept the fact that this was the new Lynn, and she was my sister, and to follow the example my father set as best I could.

I'm sure Dad had his moments of anguish, but he kept them to himself and focused on what he could control and counted his blessings. If someone suggested he get more rest, he'd invariably say he was fine, adding, "God gave me good health, this beautiful house, and a strong back for lifting Lynn."

In Longmeadow, my parents and Lynn's husband made a remarkable team effort caring for her. Her condition stayed the same for about six months, and then one day she shocked everyone when my father waved to her and she lifted one of her fingers and wagged it back at him. Hopes soared. Next there were small signs that she could either hear or read our lips when we talked. We would say the number one or two, and she would hold up the correct number of fingers. I believe Lynn's first words were "Where's Daddy?" More words soon followed, and when I came home to visit, she surprised me by saying, "Michael." Then she would close her eyes and not respond. It was as if saying one word took all her energy.

The trachea tube that helped Lynn breathe was removed, and soon the feeding tube was disconnected. We could feed Lynn, and if we were patient, over the course of an hour she could eat a small portion of baby food or food put through a blender. If we fed her too fast, she would let us know by holding up the finger on her one functioning hand to signal "Wait a minute." Around the ten-month mark, she strung together a few words and said, "I really don't know why." I think this was her way of saying she didn't know what happened to her, and soon she repeated that sentence several times a day.

Our neighbor built us a large table with a mat on it, and once a day my parents or her husband would lay Lynn on it and move her limbs. Soon she was able to bend her right knee and raise her right arm. About a year after the accident, they had her sitting in a wheelchair for a few minutes a day. Dad had a goal of Lynn walking someday, and he had railings installed in our hallway. It was an ambitious objective, because just moving Lynn from her bed to her wheelchair took real strength and a strong back. Dad developed a technique that he taught to the rest of us. First he would ever so slowly slide Lynn's legs toward the side of the bed. Then he would take her good arm, which had some strength in it, and while he was leaning over, he'd place that arm around the back of his neck. Next he bent his own knees to take some of the pressure off his back and pull her torso up to a sitting position on the side of the bed. The next move was the tricky one, because he'd straighten his back while both of his arms were around Lynn, pulling her to a standing position. She put some of her weight on her good leg, and Dad supported her while he carefully pivoted and then slowly leaned and crouched down, lowering her into the wheelchair.

I was glad I had always exercised and lifted weights at college, because transferring Lynn in and out of bed took every bit of my power and coordination. Dad, on the other hand, attributed his strength to preparation by God: "All those years of lifting bags of flour at the bakery was God's way of preparing me to work with Lynn."

Lynn's attempt to walk with the railing was a painstaking process, and whenever I did that exercise with Lynn, I realized that I was really carrying her along; without my support she would have tumbled to the ground. But we all prayed that over time this would make her one good leg stronger, and maybe someday she would be able to move around with a walker. We all had big dreams that Lynn would make a complete recovery, just like people did in the movies.

About two years after the accident, Lynn's progress stopped, and it stopped for good. Most of the time she would stare off into the unknown, and unless we actively engaged with her, she was usually unresponsive to any stimuli. Everyone worked hard to stimulate her mind. We wrote sentences for her to read and played tic-tac-toe, but if we didn't encourage her, she would just drift off in the middle of a game. She never regained the ability to have a conversation, but, oddly enough, part of her brain was sharp as a tack. Lynn could recognize pictures of people from her past and even win at tic-tac-toe. But most of the time she would either sleep or lie in bed. Her right side never regained full strength, and her left side stayed paralyzed; consequently, she would never be able to sit up or get out of bed on her own. That meant each time she had to use the toilet, she would call out, and one of us, usually my father, would repeat that Herculean task of moving her from the bed to a commode.

How he cared for Lynn through the night is beyond my comprehension, because a couple years later I gifted my parents with a stay at a nearby inn for two days and one night, providing them a short break from watching Lynn. Caring for Lynn alone was brutal, especially at night. I would just be falling asleep when she would call out for the toilet. It was a long night of never really getting any sleep, and I wondered how my father managed to follow up nights like that with days at the bakery.

Lynn's accident was like a meteor crashing into our family home, pushing us off our intended axis. It changed all our lives in so many different ways. My parents, however, did everything they could to keep day-to-day life as normal as possible, and they never put pressure on their three boys to do more for Lynn. But the simple things in life were now so much more complicated for my parents. Going out to eat required getting coverage for Lynn from a home health aide who was strong enough to lift her, and taking a vacation together was nearly impossible. But to their credit, they did not become isolated, and when they were invited over to friends' houses, they sometimes took Lynn with them. Yes, my Dad had to give up his beloved martini when he took Lynn out, but I still recall him telling his jokes and stories, even dancing. Her accident also drew Mark, Bob, and me closer together, and family, neighbors, and friends stepped up to help in so many ways. That support meant the world to our family.

That year was America's bicentennial, and I wondered if my dad would find time to continue to attend events in his minuteman garb, carrying his musket. He didn't, and when I asked about it he said something to the effect that he didn't need those hobbies as long as he had his books. "A man cannot live without books" was one of his favorite sayings, and that massive library of his provided him an escape. It wasn't uncommon for him to read the same book three of four times if he thought it was well written.

About three or four years after the accident, the company Lynn's husband worked for relocated to Florida. My parents encouraged him to go. They did not want his young life ruined, and with their blessing, Lynn's marriage to him was annulled and my parents became her sole guardians. They wanted her husband to build a new life.

For me, life had a new gravity to it, and I had deeper conversations with my parents than ever before. They would talk to me about legal and financial matters, about what should happen if they died. The accident could easily have torn the family apart, but from the beginning, both my parents were determined not to complain but rather to do the work now required of them. That set the tone for us boys, and when we were all home, we'd sit and have dinner in our usual spots, Lynn included. She was included as much as possible in day-to-day life.

My parents could easily have become bitter and withdrawn, but somehow they had the inner fortitude to be as positive as they could. I can still see my father coming home from the bakery in the late afternoon, walking slowly from his car to the back door, clearly exhausted. But when he saw Lynn, his face would light up and he'd say something like "How's my girl? You're the best." He would take a shower, the home health aide would leave, and his work of lifting, moving, and caring for Lynn would begin. I once told him how angry I was at the driver who had done this to her, and how we should sue the state for allowing him to drive without insurance. I said it wasn't fair that my father should have to work so hard and that I worried about him getting sick. He simply said, "It's an honor for me to take care of Lynn. I don't mind it at all." And he wasn't lying. Somewhere along the line, he had made a choice: Do I let my hurt and anger consume me, or do I focus on staying positive and providing a home for Lynn?

My mother had always kept her feelings to herself, guarded and reserved, and I'm sure she suffered from anguish, but she did so privately. She kept that house going and never ignored the needs of Mark, Bob or me. My mom was not one to laugh as much as my father, but I remember one sweet moment when I was home from college and showed her this new dance move called the bump. We were in the kitchen, and I swung my hips so that they bumped the refrigerator, which was my substitute for a dance partner. She asked, "Do you always need a refrigerator to do this dance?" We burst out laughing—me like a hyena and her with that body shake and muffled laugh, her hand covering her mouth.

Both parents kept their faith as well. My mother never missed a Sunday Mass, and my father would make it to his Greek Orthodox church if Mark or I was home to lift Lynn in his absence. The closest I ever saw my father question God or be resentful was when he said, "If only Lynn had left our house a few minutes later, the accident would not have happened." Another time he said, "Nixon caved in to auto executives and quashed the rule that airbags be required on all cars a couple years ago. If that coward had done the right thing, Lynn might be okay." That was the only comment I heard him say with any tinge of resentment. Otherwise he stayed upbeat, social, and simply put his head down and got the job done.

And in her own way Lynn stayed positive too. She almost never complained, and she found ways to show her appreciation. If she needed to be repositioned on the wheelchair or if her pants were riding too high, she would point to the spot, and after I fixed them, she would nod and try to smile. Every now and then we'd do something that angered her, and Lynn let us know with a guttural snarl. She might spend a whole day not saying a word, and then if my father sneezed she would surprise all of us and say, "Bless you." The smile on my father's face was priceless.

Lynn had had her own car that she called Freedom (her husband's was the one involved in the accident), and my father couldn't bear to part with it. He let Mark and me use his car, and he drove Lynn's almost exclusively. I think it was his way of staying close to her on his way to and from work.

There was no more speeding on my part, and I thought that no kid would drink and drive if they saw what had happened to Lynn. I've often felt the warnings to teenagers about alcohol and driving fall on deaf ears when they are told that you could kill yourself through dangerous driving. It implies instant death, and that has little impact. But if a teen could see how they might lose a limb or spend the rest of their life in a wheelchair, that's something they could grasp . . . and fear.

Even the commercials you see today about drunk driving tend to either highlight the chance you will be incarcerated or killed in a terrible wreck, but rarely do they interview someone who has devastating injuries. A newscast might mention there were serious injuries in a crash, but they never do a follow-up with that individual one month, one year, or ten years later. If I were to produce a short video for high school kids about the dangers of drunk driving, those people with permanent, debilitating injuries would be featured, and it just might cause a young adult to think twice and make sure someone is the designated driver. Back in 1976 the carnage from drinking and driving was more common than it is today—I lost two of my college friends to the scourge. Thank God for organizations that pushed for real change, like Mothers Against Drunk Driving.

That summer after Lynn's accident, I found solace through friendships and the outdoors. I still had plenty of impulsive, somewhat risky escapades, but they didn't involve cars. I found a new hobby: long bicycle rides. My bike became my horse, and it was the perfect activity to burn off the festering anger over Lynn's condition. While Longmeadow wasn't Vermont, being outside surrounded by green trees and blue skies was what I needed. Early rides were short and through our old neighborhood, but so many of the wooded areas we had played in as kids had been converted to housing lots, which bothered me. The Meadows, however, were protected, most of it part of the Fannie Stebbins Memorial Wildlife Refuge. I'd take long rides from our house to the Meadows and then stash the bike and take walks to our old haunts. Seeing the spot where Opie caught the big rainbow trout, where Mark and I caught our bullhead, and where I snagged the big carp gave me the feeling that at least one little slice of the outdoors would always be there in its original form—a quiet place to visit in an insane world.

CHAPTER EIGHTEEN

SENIOR YEAR AT COLLEGE FOUND ME A BIT MORE FOCUSED ON MY STUDies and making a real effort to graduate with a high grade-point average. I wanted to have the best possible chance at job offers and companies that came on campus to recruit. Unfortunately, I hadn't really assessed how my strengths could match the right type of career but instead spent the spring sending out résumés to all the companies our career placement office had contact with. And before I graduated, I landed a job with a property/casualty insurance company that would put me through a training program to become an underwriter. I really had no clue what an underwriter did—I was more concerned about showing my parents that their investment in me and Saint Michael's College was a good one and I'd be gainfully employed.

That year I'd made an effort to get down to Longmeadow more often to be with my parents and help out with Lynn, and my parents surprised me by saying they found coverage for my sister and would be at my graduation. It was a happy time, and I was especially thankful my parents never knew about the foolish rafting mishap or my near expulsion for stealing a tricycle.

After the graduation my friend Brody, who grew up in Montpelier, Vermont, invited me for a weekend of fishing. We would use Brody's dad's hunting cabin in the Worcester Range (northwest of Montpelier) as our base, and fan out to fish some of his favorite spots. I jumped at the chance, knowing that in a week I'd be starting my insurance company training in Dallas, followed by relocating to Chicago, where I would begin my career. There were no brook trout in either of those places, so one last trip to the mountains seemed the perfect end to my college days.

Brody was a far more knowledgeable trout fisherman than I, and he liked his elbow room when he fished a river. Before going to the cabin, we stopped at the Dog River; he said we'd split up and that I should go upstream to find some trout, particularly at the first bend in the river. The only advice he gave me was to move slowly and to pretend I was hunting to avoid spooking the fish. We agreed to meet back at the car in three hours.

How many days in your life have made such an impression that you can still recall virtually every detail? My walk up the river was one of the few for me. The warm May sunshine and the fresh smell of spring earth gave me a boost of energy, and I had to consciously tell myself to slow down. Although I had waders on, I did most of my walking on the bank of the river, which often took me through the woods or head-high brush. For the first half hour my casts with a Mepps spinner were ignored, and the excuses started percolating in the back of my skull: I was using the wrong lure, the water was too cold, and, finally, *This river has no fish.*

Ahead I could see the bend in the river. Water tumbled through a set of rapids and then slowed at the outside curve, where boulders and over-hanging trees provided cover. Remembering Brody's advice, I eased down into shallow water and made a sidearm cast across the river to avoid the branches reaching out from the opposite bank. The trout were tucked in on that far side, in the deep slow trough that formed up against the bank. A rainbow trout grabbed my lure and did a little cartwheel in the air, and I was able to slide him onto the sandy bank behind me. This fish, although no more than thirteen inches long, was the fattest, most colorful trout I'd ever caught—a far cry from the stocked trout my brother Bob and I caught at the fishing derby at Laurel Pond. While I gazed at its iridescent hues, something stirred inside me, indicating that this bend in the river was exactly where I was meant to be on this spring day. I became aware of the silence and that joyful feeling that can sweep over a restless soul when you are alone but not lonely.

I made my way along the river, catching another rainbow about the same size. Over time I began to recognize the difference between water that usually was devoid of trout (shallow, rapid, and sunny) and the deeper water, often near the head of pools, where the fish were. I developed a system that I still use today: Move as quickly as possible past water that did not look fishy and then take careful, crouching steps approaching what I thought was a more-productive spot. I knew I was probably passing some fish by without even casting, but what really drove me was curiosity, that *What's around the bend* quest that can be both a blessing and a curse. For me, seeing as much of the river as possible in each outing is as important as catching the fish. The yin and yang of moving fast then going into stealthy stalker mode suited me just fine.

On one of my casts, a trout followed my lure that made me gasp. The creature, probably a brown trout, looked like a submarine sizing up my offering, deciding whether it was worth risking a torpedo. The brown was probably in the nineteen-inch range, and it glided away into the depths when it was about four feet from where I was wading. It was the largest trout I'd ever seen, and a jolt of adrenaline went through me like electricity. This trout hunting was something I could get used to.

When I glanced at my watch, I did a double take. Three hours had passed since I had started fishing, but it felt like I'd been on the Dog River for less than an hour. The normal passage of time is somehow condensed when all your senses are alert and your focus is on the river and nothing else.

Instead of following the river back to Brody and our car, I took a shortcut through a freshly plowed field and found myself whistling. Puffy white clouds scudded through blue sky overhead, and it seemed this was the first time I had looked upward in a long time. I was happy and felt more alive than I had since my sister's accident. The anger of what had happened to Lynn was taking a back seat to acceptance.

Best of all, this new feeling of enjoyment did not involve alcohol or pot.

Years later I came upon a passage in a book titled *Mountain Man* written by David Marshall that eloquently described what I was feeling and what kind of man I wanted to become.

They [the mountain men] cared not at all for a dull, drab, lingering existence. They preferred to venture out rather than cower inside. They refused to let fear of death keep them from living. These men preferred an intense, exhilarating life in the wilderness, with its extremes of unbounded freedom and euphoric love of nature.

With a little luck, someday I'd have the knowledge and confidence of the mountain men I read about. But I had a long way to go.

Back at the car, Brody had two fat brown trout of seventeen inches that we'd have for our dinner the next couple of nights. Of course I had a million questions for him about fooling these big trout into biting and his technique for reading the river. And on the ride to his cabin, I soaked up his years of knowledge.

When we turned off the paved road in Worcester, Vermont, the dirt lane was so narrow I doubted two cars could pass each other, and there were little turnouts for just that purpose. So few cars traveled on the road that tufts of grass grew up from the center. As the car climbed into the hills, the road got rougher, and hemlock, birch, and maple leaned over it, jockeying for the most sunlight, forming a tunnel we passed through. Occasionally we'd pass a small house or cabin, and Brody seemed to know who lived in each one.

After what seemed like ten miles of bumping along on the rutted path, we came to its end, and that's where his cabin was. It was a two- or three-room wooden bungalow, with an outhouse out back and a water pump in the front. Night was closing in, and the temperature had already dropped into the upper thirties; we started a fire in the wood-stove, and in no time the place was snug. We sipped a couple beers, fried the trout, and found we were drowsy by nine o'clock. With no TV or radio, we soon fell asleep.

Sometime in the middle of the night, the mice woke me up. They were running above the ceiling and sounded like they were on a trampoline. Turning on my flashlight did little to slow the party down, and it was a long time before I fell back asleep. I didn't know that to be a mountain man, you had to be comfortable with an army of mice training in the rafters.

The next day we were up early, and I wanted to catch a native brook trout. Brody explained there were quite a few in a narrow stream that flowed off the mountain range, but they would be no more than six inches long at the most. That was fine with me, because the last time I caught a true native brookie was under the ice at Pollywog Pond so many years ago. I just wanted to see one again, simply to admire the unusual red dots surrounded by the blue halo on their flanks.

We found them in the stream, usually underneath where a log or branches had fallen into the water, creating a wood jam. The trout were just as beautiful as I remembered. Brody said I should come back in the fall when they spawn to see their reddish-orange bellies. Because the brook trout is actually a member of the char family, directly related to the arctic char, it held a fascination for me and still does. That was the fish featured in the childhood adventure books I read like *Cache Lake Country*, and because brookies need clear, cold water to survive, I associate them with the mountains.

As Brody and I walked out of the woods, I picked a sprig of balsam, crushed it, and held it under my nose, invigorated by the pungent scent. Balsam, brookies, moose, snowshoe hare, bobcat, and black bear all made these hills home. My desire to own a cabin came roaring back. I told myself I was dreaming, because in a week I was heading to Dallas and then to Chicago. But for now I was drinking in this rugged land and trying to stay in the moment.

We had breakfast at a local cafe, and while I'd heard Vermont accents before, it was at the restaurant where they were most pronounced. What struck me was the sound of "OY" in so many words, such as in the sentence "Hold your pipe (*pOYpe*) in all five (*fOYve*) fingers of your hand toward your side (*sOYd*) while (*wOYil*) I light it." What an odd dialect; it made me feel we were far from home.

Later, I drove Brody nuts doing my terrible imitation of the locals while he showed me the back roads. "WOYil" I wouldn't call the scenery majestic, the rolling forested hills interspersed with farms had a quiet beauty that was soothing. If it had been all farms or all forest, the effect wouldn't have been nearly as powerful, but the combination, particularly the sudden vistas at the fields, was just right.

In the towns east of Worcester, we passed lake after secluded lake that tugged at my heart. For me it was a taste of Shangri-la, and I thought that on future trips, I'd like to walk or bicycle these dirt lanes to better see the wildlife and flowers.

I found myself leaning forward in the passenger seat as we'd crest a hill to gaze into the valley below. Some of the farms had fallen on hard times, and the barns were missing a plank or two and needed a good coat of paint. On one farm, the public dirt road went right through an opening in the barn and out the other side. Driving through, we could see hay stacked in bales above us in the rafters. At another farm, the barn leaned so far to the side it looked like I could blow on it and the whole thing would topple over onto the black-and-white Holstein cows inside.

As we drove I thought about the location for my imaginary cabin. Brody's cabin was fine, but I knew my place needed to be on or near a lake or river for swimming. The land had to have some kind of view, a place where I could stare off into the distance. I mentioned this to Brody, and he suggested I think in terms of buying land, camping on it, and building later. It was an idea worth considering—when and if I ever returned from the upcoming job in Chicago.

That night back at Brody's cabin, I started reading a book I'd brought with me: *Living the Good Life* by Helen and Scott Nearing. They had left an urban area and bought a few acres and an old house in rural Vermont in 1932, where they stayed for twenty years before moving to another plot of land in Maine. Like the David Grayson books, this one seemed to find me at just the right time in my life.

Different readers will come away with different messages from the Nearings' book, but what I remember most is that by living frugally and simply, they enjoyed a healthy and independent life. The couple grew most of their own food, raising a little money via cash crops and writing articles, often securing what they needed through bartering. They were always participants and never spectators, and their lifestyle reminded me of Louise Dickinson Rich (*We Took to the Woods*) and Bradford Angier (*We Like It Wild*). The Nearings enjoyed hard work because they were their own bosses. They were in control, were content, and seemed to have a strong marriage. Scott Nearing once said that if he was given a bunch of money, there was nothing he could think of that he'd buy, and that he really didn't want or need the money. Now that was a mindset that appealed to me. I knew I could work just as hard as they did, but there were still some creature comforts I aspired to. Maybe someday I'd find the right balance and be as gratified as the Nearings.

Back in Longmeadow, I told my dad about the trip, and he seemed truly interested, or maybe he knew that I'd be leaving for Dallas soon and so made the effort to carve out time for me. His days of traveling were reduced by his mission of helping Lynn, so he lived vicariously through the explorations of Mark, Bob, and me. I explained that I was going to save as much money as I could from the new job so that someday I could buy a new car or maybe even the cabin. He certainly liked the sound of that, because for as long as I can remember, in a variety of different ways, he imparted the message of "It's not how much you make but how much you keep."

It was good advice for a twenty-two-year-old about to set off into parts unknown.

CHAPTER NINETEEN

DALLAS, TEXAS. UPON ARRIVAL I FELT I HAD LANDED ON A DIFFERENT planet. A furnace blast of scorching-hot June air hit me like a punch, more powerful than the ovens at the bakery. Boarding a taxi I looked out the window at four or five lanes of traffic snaking through the flattest place I'd ever seen. Urban and suburban sprawl stretched out in all directions. The shock of coming from the shady dirt roads of northern Vermont to the Dallas–Fort Worth metroplex, where a quarter of all Texans live, was disconcerting to say the least. I wondered what people did on the weekends without nearby rivers, lakes, and hills to explore. I soon found out.

A Ramada Inn would be my home for the next two months while I attended training classes. Thank God it had a pool and I was lucky enough to have a good roommate, a fellow trainee named Dave. I figured those two pluses would see me through my stay, and I'd put all my time and energy into learning my new job and the culture of the company that hired me. But, true to form, I did neither. A girl in my training class consumed most of my attention. We hit it off, and perhaps we might have ended up together for the long run—except for one little problem. Her wedding was scheduled the week after training class ended. And so this would be a fling, and it would get me into a bit of trouble, like so many romances in the past and so many yet to come.

Before I took this job I discussed it with my parents. I was hoping to find work closer to Longmeadow so I could help with Lynn. My parents encouraged me to go. They assured me they would be fine and that a young man should venture out in the world, see new places, and learn new skills. Besides, this was the only job offer I had, and they were delighted for me.

Looking back, I think I enjoyed every minute I was in Dallas. It was not the kind of place a mountain/water lover like me could ever call home, but it certainly had an active nightlife. I thought the people there lived quite differently from New Englanders. The restaurants and bars were always packed, and it made me wonder if Texans ever ate a meal in their own homes. We trainees certainly added to the local economic hospitality industry, because we were all on expense accounts, something quite different from the frugal living I thought I'd practice after reading the Nearings' book. But, hey, I couldn't keep the expense account money (I had to provide receipts), so I figured I might as well enjoy myself, and that's what I did. From barbecue to Mexican food, from cowboy bars to strip bars, I made it my business to see as much of the city as I could.

It seemed half the people in Dallas were from somewhere else, making them more outgoing than New Englanders, and everyone I met seemed to be having a party or a cookout. At one of these parties I met a seventeen-year-old named Ramsey, who said he was a pilot. I laughed, thinking he was bullshitting me, but over the course of several beers I realized he was telling the truth. His plane of choice was a glider, and he explained that no matter how late he stayed at the party, he was getting up early the next morning to go flying. Would I like to come?

Of all the crazy things I'd done, this one seemed middle of the road. After all, I figured if a seventeen-year-old knew how to fly a plane, he must be quite smart and know all the rules.

I stayed at the party into the wee hours of the morning then crawled back to the hotel in time to get a couple hours' sleep before my alarm went off shortly after dawn. Using the company car, I drove to a remote airport. It must have been eighty-five degrees already under a piercing sun, still low in the sky. Ramsey was waiting (I never found out if it was his first name or last), and so was the white-and-red glider on the runway. I'd never seen one up close, and it looked sleek yet flimsy, with incredibly long wings that appeared as though they could be blown off by a stiff breeze. I wondered why there was a long line going from the nose of the glider to another aircraft with an engine in front of us.

"How else do you think we get up?" queried Ramsey, as if to an imbecile. Then I realized we were going to be towed down the runway, and continue being towed up into the sky.

"Kid Pilot Ramsey," as I thought of him, wasn't much on instructions. There were two seats in the plane, one directly in front of the other in the narrow cockpit. The forward seat was literally inches away from the nose of the aircraft. Ramsey pointed for me to climb into the front one. As I stepped up to my seat, I thought, *Good thing I'm little; this thing is not designed for large folks.* Once I was wedged in, he got in the back, closed the clear plastic hatch cover, and a bit of claustrophobia came over me. But that was nothing compared to the heat—I was sitting inside a tiny greenhouse, baking in the sun. I was going to ask Kid Pilot to turn on the air-conditioning if there was any, but the next thing I knew we were being towed down the runway.

The drone of the engine and the wind made me think the plane pulling us was straining, but it did the job, and the glider's wheels lifted from the ground. We climbed ever higher, and with clear skies, a couple puffy clouds, and a pancake landscape, I felt I could see all the way to Oklahoma. I wasn't sure I liked being in the front seat, as I could see only the tip of the nose of the aircraft and no other parts of the plane; it felt like being towed to the heavens in a plastic bubble.

Suddenly it was quiet. Kid Pilot had released from the towrope, and now we were soaring on our own. I had controls in front of me, and I thought, *He's a pretty trusting guy to assume I'm mature enough not to touch them.* My next thought was *I'm a pretty trusting guy to go flying with a seventeen-year-old I met the night before while drunk at a party.*

Ramsey seemed capable enough, because we were climbing higher in a thermal. Then he cut out from the spiral and started doing a few dips. My stomach was in my throat for a minute, but I was enjoying myself. Kid Pilot tapped on the plastic cover, and I gave a thumbs-up. That was my mistake.

Now the ride became alarming as he banked the plane so sharply I thought I'd fall out. Beads of perspiration had turned into rivulets of sweat streaming from every pore in my body. Ramsey gave me a couple moments to recover as he built up speed soaring in a straight line. I don't really know what he did next. It was an abrupt and violent motion, so I shut my eyes. To this day I don't know if it was a roll, a loop, or a spiral dive, but between the motion and the heat, I was about to upchuck. That would not be a good thing in a one-hundred-degree plastic bubble.

I opened my eyes just as he did another maneuver, where all I could see was blue sky below me and the barren scrub to my upper left. Then we plunged for a few seconds before straightening out.

I gave a thumbs-down sign that I wanted to land. By now I thought this kid was crazy—it seemed like we were coming toward the parched brown earth at much too steep an angle and I'd be squished like a bug on impact. At the last minute he pulled the nose up and we eased down onto the dirt runway for a bumpy but safe landing.

When the glider came to a stop and Ramsey opened the hatch, I stumbled out of the cockpit and puked.

"You OK?" Kid Pilot asked in his drawl.

"Just fine, just fine. Too many beers last night." I didn't want him to think we New England hillbillies were babies.

"That was one of my best rides ever," he said.

"Well thanks, but I gotta go. I need to bring the company car back so the rest of the class can use it."

I never saw Ramsey again, and I don't know exactly what happened up there. I have not been in a glider since.

The eight weeks in Dallas went by in a blur, and I failed to do the very thing I set out to do, which was learn the skill set required for my new job. It all had to do with being preoccupied with the girl I met and my inability to say no to anything and everything. At least, I thought, if my life ends soon, I won't be lying in some hospital bed saying I should have had more fun or done this or that. It would be easy to cite Lynn's accident as the reason I lived like there was no tomorrow and said yes to every interesting opportunity that came my way, but the truth is I was probably born that way—the accident just cemented that mindset.

The girl I was in love with said goodbye after I asked a hundred times if she was sure she wanted to go through with her upcoming marriage. She said it was too late, that she would shatter everyone if she did that. I answered with "What about me? What about you? You wouldn't be with me if he was the right guy."

But the die was cast. She flew to New York and I to Chicago.

As far as cities go, I liked Chicago. Our office was in the Loop business district, on the twenty-sixth floor of a high-rise. A sea of desks for us worker bees sprawled in every direction, and the managers had offices around the edges. Consequently, they got the great views out the windows, and the rest of us could either look at one another or at the paper files that were stacked on each underwriter's desk or in cabinets. In 1977 there were no personal computers, so almost all our transactions were done on the phone or by mail, and paper was everywhere. The strangest thing I remember is that you could smoke a cigarette at your desk, which about half the office did. So it's unsurprising what happened shortly after my arrival.

I'd been in Chicago two weeks, just getting to know some of my fellow office workers, when my phone rang at 6:00 a.m. A woman from work explained that there had been a small fire in our office and that I should come in but wear old clothes. Quite an odd request, but I was the new guy and did as I was told. Maybe there were some wet spots on the floor in the section where the fire had been and she didn't want us ruining our good shoes and pants.

When I got off the train and walked to our building, there were fire trucks still below the high-rise. I glanced up at the twenty-sixth floor and did a double take. Half the windows were missing.

Incredibly, the elevators were operating normally, and I rode one up. When the door opened, all I could see was black. Then a fireman walked by and said something to the effect that I could come out; everything was safe. I gingerly stepped from the elevator, not at all sure that the burned-out floor was harmless. The smell of smoke, charcoal really, was overpowering. Someone had strung a few bare lights toward the back of the cavernous room in the section where my desk was, and I headed that way. My guess about water on the floor was correct, but I wasn't prepared for the charred files, the burned-out ceiling, and the broken windows.

When I got to my desk I almost laughed. *Why the hell did they call us into the office?* My phone had melted over the top of my desk, and everything that wasn't steel had burned. Ash covered the entire mess. *What the hell did they expect me to do?*

A few minutes later my supervisor walked in. He shuffled over, and—I am not making this up—lit a cigarette. Gone was his professional demeanor, replaced by a *I don't give a damn anymore* attitude.

"These idiots called us in for this?" he muttered.

Others started filtering in, and their reaction was much the same. Finally the head honcho arrived, gathered us around, and told us our job was to look for files that hadn't been burned and put them in rows by the elevator. We bitched and moaned but did as we were told.

Oddly, in that one day of sifting through charred files, I met more potential friends than I had the entire two weeks. Everyone's guard was down, and people seemed to act differently in blue jeans than they did in a suit and tie or a dress.

Over the next two weeks we relocated to another floor, and by that time I'd met many people in their twenties and formed friendships. It was especially fun because about 40 percent of the office was Black and the rest white, and the fire gave us all an opportunity to get to know one another much better than if we were chained to our desks. During this period we all went out to lunch, and I even announced I was having a party at my apartment that weekend. I worried that no one would show up, but by 9:00 p.m. the place was packed. People reciprocated, and from that time onward I had an active social life. In fact two girls, Terrie and Brenda, lived on the north shore, and they gave me the run of their apartment on the weekends so I didn't have to drive back to the suburbs. I started bringing my bicycle into the city, and found that on Saturday and Sunday mornings I could ride along the lakefront with few pedestrians to dodge.

The writer in me was also showing signs of life, because I started writing long stories about incidents like the fire and sending photocopies to my parents (which, fortunately, my mother saved; I still have them). My parents wrote back and said they were going to find coverage for Lynn and fly out for a quick visit. I also wrote letters to Bob and Mark and, maybe because both of them are artistic, started sketching different outdoor scenes and sent a couple to Bob. One of the sketches was of my imaginary cabin. I still have the picture. It shows a one-room cabin on a hilltop overlooking a pond ringed by mountains. A long driveway leads up to the cabin, passing beneath towering maples. In the woods to the left of the driveway is a stream coming down through hemlocks.

I didn't know it at the time, but sketching out whatever it is you desire is one way to help manifest its arrival. All I knew was that the sketch was one of longing, and I could actually feel myself sitting on the little deck I drew extending out from the cabin and over the hillside above the pond.

—◦—

Workdays in 1977 were so much different than today. You worked 9–5, had an hour for lunch, and even had a morning break when a cafeteria lady would come around with a cart carrying doughnuts and coffee. I must have had plenty of free time on my hands, because I even volunteered to coach a team of floor hockey players in the recreational league where I lived. The kids were ages ten to twelve, and this was my first coaching experience. The first practice was a disaster—the kids took advantage of my lack of experience and ran wild. During a scrimmage, no one stayed in their positions, and all the players wanted to chase after the puck. There was one funny moment when a slap shot went flying into the boy's bathroom and we heard a scream. One of our players came running out trying to hold up his pants.

We got blown out in our first game, so during the next practice I held a team meeting and talked to the players as if they were adults, explaining why each of them needed to cover their section of the floor and that not all of them were going to score goals. Little by little we got better, and later in life I coached students for many years and loved the experience.

My apartment was out in a suburb where I roomed with Dave, the same hotel roommate I had in Dallas. We'd take the train into work, and I'd gaze out the window to get a feel for the area, disappointed to see it was wall-to-wall suburban homes without a patch of woods anywhere. The streets were so tightly packed, I didn't spot any that would be attractive for biking, and I realized I'd have to use my car to find some woodsy places to reconnect with nature. Long before the term "nature deficit disorder" was coined, I began to recognize that's what I was suffering from after living in Dallas and now Chicago. I felt restless and a little despondent for no apparent reason—kind of like a caged animal. As I sat looking out the train window, I vowed to spend part of each weekend outdoors and save part of every check, no matter how small, to someday buy that cabin I'd been dreaming about.

Some weekends I'd drive south, north, and west looking for a clear river to fish, but I never found one. It wasn't until I ventured far north into Wisconsin that I found terrain somewhat similar to Vermont. Back at the office I organized a weekend canoe trip to Wisconsin. Most of my coworkers were city people, but they were game for the adventure, and more than one canoe capsized as we paddled down a river. But my lasting memory is how friendly the people in Wisconsin are. After our canoe trip, we all went to a local pub. We had a great time but arrived back at our campsite in the dark, and we had yet to set up our tents. A few of us fumbled around with a tiny flashlight, while others just spread out their sleeping bags and fell asleep. Headlights came bumping down the road toward our site, and I thought it would be the police because our "campsite" was simply a turn-off by the river. There were multiple cars, and they weren't the police, so I grew wary, thinking that whoever these people were, they were looking for a fight. Instead they turned out to be the folks we met in the pub, who said they had a suspicion we might need help at our campsite. They then set up our tents in the glow of their car headlights!

My desire to have more weekends in the countryside led me to my next misadventure, which ranks near the top of the "Ten Dumbest Things Mike Did."

A woman named Shelly, who worked in my company's auditing department, had caught my eye, and I asked her out. She politely turned me down, saying she had a longtime boyfriend back in her home state of Michigan. I figured that was the end of it, but one evening she showed up at my apartment unannounced; one thing led to another, and we ended up in bed. Soon we were spending a lot of evenings together without considering what her boyfriend might have thought about it.

About three weeks later, Shelly asked if I wanted to go and see the comedian Steve Martin, who was performing at a college in Michigan. She said it would be too far a drive to just go for one night and that we should go for a weekend, stay at a cabin on a beautiful lake, and I could spend some of the time fishing.

"I'm there!" I said. Steve Martin, a cabin, and fishing—what's not to like! But the devil is in the details, and Shelly, somewhat casually, added that the cabin belonged to her boyfriend.

Now a normal person would have squashed the whole idea immediately, but I wasn't normal, and Shelly was convincing in a conniving sort of way. She explained that while she hadn't exactly gotten around to breaking up with her boyfriend, she likely would down the road, but on this trip she and I would be traveling as friends.

The ping-pong ball in my head went back and forth: boyfriend versus Steve Martin/cabin/fishing. Guess which won? I was blinded by the thoughts of staying in a cabin in the woods and didn't think the situation through to its potentially violent climax.

The Steve Martin show was everything I hoped it would be, the cabin was deep in the woods, and the lake was spring-fed with good fishing. I met Shelly's boyfriend, who was an interesting guy: a big-time hunter, fisherman, and outdoorsman. Under different circumstances, we might have become friends. He worked in construction and had a roommate to help pay the bills. The roommate was a nice guy who I did get to know, and we fished together the second evening. Shelly and her boyfriend went out to visit friends, leaving me at the cabin with the roommate.

Around 9:00 p.m. the phone at the cabin rang. The roommate picked it up, but I was sitting in the same room and could hear his side of the conversation. Here is my best recollection of what I heard:

"She did what?"

Pause.

"You're kidding me."

Pause

"It's really all over?"

Long pause.

"What? With *him*?"

Longer pause . . . while the roommate glared at me.

I stood up and, in true Woody Allen fashion, pointed at myself while mouthing, *Me?*

The roommate nodded then said into the phone: "OK, OK, calm down; there's no need for violence."

I stopped listening and felt light-headed for a moment before scooting into my guest room, where I threw my stuff into my travel bag. When I came out of my room, the roommate was off the phone.

"Oh shit, man!" he yipped, looking at me. "He's on his way back here. Shelly broke up with him, and she told him everything. How could you!"

There was no time to answer. I sprinted to that shitbox car of mine, the Datsun B-210, and thank God it started. I'd like to say I screeched out of the driveway, but this was the car that came to a stop when five people were in it on a steep hill. I then proceeded to get totally lost on a maze of back roads. The few times headlights came my way, I either expected a shot to ring out or the other car to block my path.

When you know you're in the wrong, you certainly don't feel like fighting. All your adrenaline is in the flight response, not the fight one. I spent half that night trying to find my way out of Michigan, and didn't get back to my apartment until seven o'clock the next morning. In the end, all I lost was the fishing rod I left behind . . . and a bit of my pride.

———

My parents did come and visit a few months later, and I look back and think how lucky I was that they flew all the way to Chicago, even though they could only stay one night. But they were in great spirits when I picked them up at the airport. We drove straight into the city. My mom wanted to see where I worked, and my dad wanted to visit a submarine—a U-boat to be more precise. Housed at the Museum of Science and Industry, it was the only U-boat in the United States.

I was hoping we'd go to a Cubs game, but I put on my best face, and once at the museum became enthralled with *U-505*, which was captured by the US Navy in 1944. The living quarters, the control room, the galley, and the hallways were so tight it was hard to comprehend that up to fifty-five men lived and served inside this claustrophobic steel cylinder. Dad knew all about the history of this particular sub without reading the museum literature, and as we toured he commented so that I could understand how the U-boat operated. It must have had an effect on me, because forty years later I co-wrote a book about its sister ship, *U-506*, which was one of the first German subs to go all the way to the mouth of the Mississippi River. *See, Dad, I was listening.* This was one of the "Ten Smartest Things Mike Did." Not just writing the book but, way back in 1978, going along with my dad's idea to tour the sub and not trying to persuade him to see a Cubs game.

It was shortly after my parents left that I reached what I thought at the time was a monumental decision. I remember exactly where I was when I made it: standing on the train platform in Arlington Heights, Illinois. It was a fine spring day, and trees had just begun to leaf out. It reminded me of the day on the Dog River, just one year earlier, when I caught the fat rainbows.

When the train pulled up, I climbed inside, the door closed behind me, and I said to myself, *Time to go home.*

CHAPTER TWENTY

I WAS FORTUNATE THAT MY COMPANY HAD AN OFFICE OUTSIDE Boston, and they transferred me there in September 1978. Old friends such as Opie, Dale, Cogs, Booge, Griff, Gusto, and I all reconnected. Dale and I, along with a couple guys from work, rented a big house in Needham, Massachusetts.

Although I missed my friends in Chicago (even Shelly), being back in New England not only gave me a chance to have my closest friends around but also allowed me to make frequent trips to Longmeadow and spend time with my family. Lynn's condition had not changed—nor would it ever—but my parents had adapted as best they could. Instead of having a feeling of dread when I went home, I looked forward to it. I did worry about the toll Lynn's care was taking on my father and urged him to retire from the bakery. He said he wasn't ready just yet, and when I pushed him to explain why, he snapped at me: "I don't want or need you to worry about me! I'm doing just fine. Lots of people do something just like Jerri and I do for Lynn."

After living in greater Chicago, I had a hankering for mountains, clear streams, spruce, and fir and made a trip to northern Vermont that autumn. I went alone, which my friends thought odd, but I was taking note of my preferences and realized I liked people best after I'd been away from them for a short period.

Once in Vermont I got a room in a cheap hotel and was up early the next morning to fish the Dog River. I recalled the trip with Brody and how I didn't have enough time to fish some deep pools that were behind a house in the woods surrounded by a chain-link fence. Inside that chain-link fence was a Doberman pinscher, letting me know who owned the place.

Now I was back at the fence in the gray dawn. It had rained the prior day, and the river was too deep and swift to wade, but the fence blocked my path. I just knew the deep pools held "submarine trout" like the one I saw on my first trip. The Doberman was nowhere to be seen. What to do?

I held the fishing rod in my teeth, biting down on the cork handle, and ever so slowly climbed the fence. Lowering myself down the other side, I came to a complete stop, hearing only the pounding of my heart. If the snarling dog attacked, I figured I had enough time to get back up and over the fence. I waited two or three minutes, my eyes covering as much ground as possible. Nothing moved, and I surmised the dog was inside the house.

Technically, I was trespassing, but it incensed me that someone could block my path to the river with a fence. However, the last time I had gone over a chain-link fence—as a little kid—the result had not been a pleasant one. That was warning #1. I'd been raised to follow the rules, and here I was clearly breaking at least one. Warning #2. Still, I decided to cross the yard and get to the river.

Looking back, I now realize that despite my newfound closeness with my father, we approached some decisions quite differently, and that would never change. Taking calculated risks was part of my DNA. I was well aware that if the Doberman charged out of the gloom, I was on my own.

I'm pleased to report that I made it to the river safely, and was correct about the pools holding big fish. Two giant brown trout were in shallow water next to the bank of the river, feeling safe in their early-morning habit of patrolling the edges of the pool for crayfish. (Almost every large brown trout I've ever caught and kept had at least one crayfish in its stomach.)

The problem with seeing trout, however, is that if you can see them, they have surely spotted you, and the two big fish I located glided off into the depths. I only caught three small fish that morning, but I couldn't wait to come back and try for those monster browns again. I'd find another way to access those pools rather than tempting fate with the Doberman, or perhaps I'd find even better pools farther upstream. I realized it would take many trips to cover all the twists and turns of this twenty-mile-long river, and that got me to thinking that this region of Vermont would be a good place to try to buy the cabin I craved. The area had the advantage of not being close to a ski area, where the prices would be much higher. On the other hand, a cabin here would be a four-hour drive from my apartment in Boston, but I figured the long drive would be worth it because there was less development here than in southern Vermont.

Back at my apartment I began the first tentative steps toward researching property costs. With no internet in 1978, I reviewed classified ads in the newspapers and called several Realtors. I soon found that ten thousand dollars was about the minimum price for a small cabin and four or five acres in northern Vermont. That certainly doesn't sound like a lot by today's standards, but it was double the amount of money I had saved, and I didn't know what a mortgage was.

One weekend at my parents' house, I talked to them about my goal of buying a cabin and my money situation. They'd been listening to this dream for many years, but this was the first conversation where I explained I'd done research and that I'd saved five thousand dollars. Just an hour after I was done discussing my situation, my father shocked me by saying he had spoken with my mother and they would match my five thousand dollars with a loan of the same amount. They could have pointed me toward a mortgage but instead were probably thinking of my long-term financial security. A loan from them at no interest and one I could pay back in five years was certainly generous—especially because I knew that with their commitment to Lynn, they would not be able to use the cabin. Besides, a remote cabin was the last place on earth my mother would want to go. But I think they felt our family could use a boost, and they knew Mark and Bob would enjoy the cabin almost as much as I would.

Now the dream was within reach. Each time a Realtor called me about a potential place, I studied topographical maps to pinpoint its location and see how close it was to a river or a lake. And each time I came away disappointed. Realtors explained that lakefront property was usually beyond my budget, and that riverfront land had its own set of challenges, the biggest one being the potential for flooding.

A couple of the classifieds describing property on or near water looked promising, and I called the owners directly. Again I came away disappointed, usually because the property was only an acre and had neighbors on either side. That was hardly the mountain-man lifestyle I yearned for.

I quickly learned to put my requirements in writing: four acres minimum of land, a small cabin (plumbing and electricity not required), a secluded setting, and on or near a river or lake. Just as quickly, I realized that many Realtors ignored my requests and would call me with property that was missing one of those key ingredients. Or, even worse, they would say, "The cabin is on a beautiful trout stream," but when I talked to owners they'd explain that was a stretch—the stream was seasonal and went down to a trickle in summer.

A couple months went by, and it seemed I was destined to buy land and build a cabin later. Then, on December 20, I received a phone call from a Realtor that got me excited. She described six wooded acres on a ridge that had a partially completed cabin (which she and all Vermonters refer to as a "camp") at the highest point on the land. Best of all, it overlooked a pond of about thirty acres, and the land had about two hundred feet of pond frontage. During our phone call I got the feeling that this was an honest Realtor, not one to exaggerate, as so many had done before her. She was straightforward and said that even in summer the dirt lane going up to the hill was too rough for a car to climb. Did I have a truck, she asked, with four-wheel drive? No, I answered, I had a crappy Datsun B-210 that came to a stop on steep hills . . . when the car was not in the shop.

"I'm telling you about the road," she said, "because if you come up, you won't be able to see it. It's covered with three feet of snow."

Holy cow, I thought; *it's a whole different world up there.* At my apartment we had six inches of snow.

But instead of turning me off, the amount of snow and the bad road intrigued me. Here was a cabin in the north country, far off the beaten path, and even farther off the town-maintained dirt road.

Then the Realtor mentioned two more pieces of information I liked. The cabin was listed for eighty-five hundred dollars, and she could show it to me immediately. She said she had extra snowshoes for me to wear.

"I think," she added, "the camp and land are offered at a very fair price. If you are really interested in it, you would probably have to act within the next week."

I explained that the only day I could be there was the day before Christmas. Undeterred, she gave me directions to meet her at a general store at 2:00 p.m.

That Christmas Eve day was a cold one. When I arrived at the general store, at the intersection of two dirt roads in northern Vermont, the temperature was fifteen degrees. The Realtor, a middle-aged woman named Cecilia, was already waiting. We shook hands, and she suggested that I follow her in my car, explaining that when we couldn't drive any farther, we'd strap on snowshoes and hike up the ridge to the cabin. She mentioned that I might want to be alone up there and walk around after she showed me the cabin, and that's why we would take two cars.

The dirt roads we traveled had been plowed, but there was still an inch or two of hard-packed snow covering them. Cecilia drove slowly, knowing I did not have four-wheel drive. Soon she pulled over, and we parked our cars and strapped on snowshoes. The air and snow were so dry, our snowshoes sometimes made squeaking sounds as we trudged up what appeared to be a logging road winding high into the hills. An occasional snowflake drifted down from a leaden sky. Although I started to perspire from the exertion, it was a pleasant climb through a forest of mostly beech and maple trees. As we walked, Cecelia pointed through the woods to the left, explaining that the property extended in that direction for about a hundred feet, just short of a tiny brook. To the right, she explained, the property went beyond the crest of the ridge then down a steep hill to the pond.

We rested a moment while we caught our breath, and I used the opportunity to ask who owned the cabin and property. She explained that a farmer who had a big spread about forty-five minutes to the south was the owner and that he was the one who had started construction on the camp. I asked why he stopped the work and decided to sell, and she explained that he needed to raise some cash. She thought he might have been building the camp to use during deer hunting season.

We continued up the lane, and when Cecilia encouraged me not to be slowed down by her, I increased my strides. Under all that snow, I had no idea what condition the "driveway" was in other than Cecilia's description that it was in rough shape and only a four-wheel-drive vehicle could navigate it. At the very top of the ridge, I got my first view of the cabin—an A-frame with a tar-paper roof. It was about forty feet long by twenty-five feet wide and rested atop cinder blocks, which formed a nice little cave-like area that I hoped no black bear had found. I noted how the snow had slid off the roof and formed giant piles on either side. The front of the cabin had a three-foot-wide porch with a broken railing on its outer edge. There was one window on the second floor and another window and a door on the first floor.

The wood framing across the front of the building was either unpainted or white, indicating that the owner had used scrap wood to form that outside wall. Two white birches grew directly in front of the porch, their branches extending over the peak of the A-frame. Giant hemlocks and towering spruce crowded in from the back and the sides. In front of the cabin, however, was a flat clearing of about sixty feet by thirty feet.

The cabin was perched at the very edge of the ridge, and Cecilia wasn't exaggerating that it was a steep drop down to the pond. Not quite a cliff, but close. That sloping hillside—about 250 feet in length—was thick with trees, blocking any view of the pond. I climbed the two steps onto the porch and, looking northwest, could make out a mountain range far in the distance. Not a sound could be heard. At that moment, I was sold on the place.

Cecelia came tramping up the hill and stood on the porch next to me, catching her breath. A couple minutes passed and she said, "Nice and secluded. Ready to go inside?"

The door wasn't locked because someone had broken a small pane of glass that was part of the door. There was a piece of wood where the glass should have been, and anyone who wanted to enter the cabin could just push that wood out, reach inside, and turn the knob. Cecilia didn't know if someone had broken inside or the owner simply didn't bother with a lock.

Inside the cabin it was gloomy, with gray light coming in from the window in the front and one in the back. It felt much colder inside than the fifteen degrees outside. Cecilia turned on a light, and it dawned on me that I hadn't even asked if the cabin had electricity; now I was thrilled that it did. The walls were just bare two-by-fours for the framing, with no insulation, drywall, or wood covering. A sink stood under the front window, but Cecilia said there was no well, plumbing, or septic. She explained that an outhouse stood about fifty feet behind the cabin.

An image of me lugging a five-gallon water jug up that long driveway flashed through my mind, but I was young and healthy and thought I could manage it. Bathing would have to be in the pond.

Up against the back wall was a dilapidated couch, but next to it were four handcrafted oak chairs with wide armrests. I sat in one and exclaimed, "This chair is a beauty, comfortable and sturdy." Cecilia said she could picture me sitting on the little porch in it.

We lowered a set of pull-down stairs from the ceiling, and I climbed to the second floor. Strips of wood lay all over place, and the ceiling above had been partly insulated. Mice had obviously been having a grand old time on this second floor, and it needed a thorough cleaning.

Back on the first floor, I wondered out loud why there was no woodstove, and Cecilia said they simply hadn't gotten around to it. She surmised that all the time the owner had spent at the camp was likely working: constructing the driveway and building the cabin.

I took one last look around the first floor and thought I could make it livable despite my lack of carpentry skills. All it really needed was insulation and then some type of wood or paneling to cover the walls and ceiling. Outside needed a coat of paint, and I was already wondering how I would reach the peaks of the A-frame to get them painted.

We stepped back out onto the porch and closed the door behind us. Cecilia was smart. She had let the land do the talking and could see how interested I was.

"Would you mind," I asked, "if I snowshoe down to the pond and have a look around?"

"Not at all. It's going to take you a while, so why don't you meet me back at my car. That way I can get warm with the car's heater."

The hill was so steep I had to do a sidestep down it with the snow-shoes or zigzag when possible. I'm not sure what I expected to see because the pond was iced-over and covered with snow. It took a while getting down, and I thought how my first job would be to create a proper path to the water. Two ice fisherman were set up in the center of the pond. Not a single cabin could be seen along the pond's wooded shore. It occurred to me that the layout of this property was almost exactly like the picture I had sketched a year earlier, even down to the curves in the driveway leading up the hill. Did I subconsciously decide this was the place for me because it looked like the drawing, or did I somehow manifest into reality what I wanted? There was no way of knowing.

After standing and trying to visualize what the pond would be like during a summer swim, I scaled back up the hill. Snowflakes started coming down in earnest, and they made a hissing sound in the trees. This side of the ridge faced north, and instead of the maples and beeches that grew along the driveway, the hill was cloaked with spruce, hemlock, balsam fir, and white birch. Two white pines towered over all of them. On my way up I almost turned around and went back to the pond to ask the ice fishermen if they knew how deep it was, but I'd already kept Cecilia waiting. I was gambling that a pond of thirty acres had some depth to it.

When I reached the crest of the ridge and the cabin I was smiling. I'm not a religious person, but I do have a spiritual side, and I always felt closer to God or a Higher Power when I was in his creation rather than man's. My ADD and hyperactivity had been diminishing over the years, and in nature that feeling often left me altogether. I visualized myself sitting on the cabin porch, just like Cecilia said, and feeling closer to the Great Creator than ever before. The cabin had the potential to bring a larger peace into my life.

As I caught my breath after snowshoeing up the hill, I was already prioritizing what tasks I'd do to make the place my own. One of the most important would be to thin some trees on the hillside so I could at least see a glimmer of sparkling blue water come summertime. I laugh now, thinking how I envisioned cutting the trees by ax and then cutting them further into cordwood size for the woodstove I planned to install when I got the money. Hacking away at a full-size tree with an ax is a job and a half, and I marvel that the colonial settlers had the stamina to keep at it day after day.

—◦—

I rendezvoused with Cecilia at her car and greeted her with "I'll buy it." I didn't even know you could negotiate the price, but maybe that ignorance served me well, not allowing another buyer to come in to look at and possibly take the property. We sat in her warm car, and I signed a couple documents and gave her a small check as a down payment. She gave me the name of a local attorney to do the title search, and then commented on the snow coming down and suggested I head for home. I nodded. She gave me directions on how to reach a paved road that would lead toward Montpelier, and we shook hands goodbye. Then, without snowshoes, I walked a short ways down the county road onto the snow-covered ice of the pond, and slogged along the shoreline toward my land.

The words "my land" or something to that effect rattled around in my thoughts, and I was elated. The thrill of first-time ownership was like a drug, and I ignored the swirling snow and instead looked at the ridge like a king surveying his kingdom. My eyes were on the different trees crowding the shoreline, looking for a place on my property where I could hack out a little beach area and build a dock.

It was getting close to dusk, and I finally retraced my steps to my car, waving at the ice fisherman, who were packing up their gear. I wondered if they had caught trout, perch, or bass, but with the snow now coming down hard, I was anxious to start the lengthy drive to Longmeadow.

Hopping in my car, I started the engine to warm it up, eating a candy bar and drinking half-frozen water. I pointed the car toward home, gave the gas pedal a gentle push, and promptly skidded off the road. The front of the car had slid down a two-foot embankment into a ditch, and the rear of the car stuck out at a right angle to the road. I tried putting the battered Datsun into reverse, but the wheels just spun without gaining purchase.

My spirits plummeted from the high of buying the cabin, and now I wondered how I'd ever get home. There were no cell phones back then, and the only house I could see was a shack with no car out front and no woodsmoke coming from the chimney. The falling snow and cold temperature reminded me that this situation could turn serious if I didn't get help fast.

That's when I ran along the road back toward the pond, hoping the ice fishermen hadn't left. I found them at their truck and asked for their help. The driver was short and stocky, looking about my age, and his partner was tall with a gray-flecked beard. Luckily, they took pity on this sad-sack flatlander; all three of us hopped in their truck and drove to my car, inspecting the mess I'd gotten myself into.

The taller of the two men said, "God damn Jeezum, no wonder you're in a pickle, you ain't got no chains on those little tires." *Yep*, I felt like saying, *that's me, the man with no chains and even less common sense.* Instead I answered him with a question. "Do you think the three of us could push it out?"

"Naw," said the shorter one, who wore overalls covered with grease and a smattering of what I hoped was fish blood. "We got a chain in the back of the truck; we'll hitch it to your car and yank it out."

They did so in record time. I couldn't thank them enough, and the taller one gave me these words of wisdom: "You really ought to break down and buy some chains."

I said that was good advice. As he was rolling up the truck window, I said, "Wait a minute."

He rolled the window down with his right hand and tugged on his beard with his left, eyeing me, perhaps suspiciously or perhaps the way he did for any moron he came across.

"Just had to ask you, what did you catch in the pond?"

"The usual, a few perch and a couple smallmouth bass."

"One last question. Do you know how deep the pond is?"

"Forty-five feet at its deepest. Spring fed and brook fed. You plan on coming back?"

"Hope to. Thanks for your help."

It took much longer than I thought to find the paved road, and night closed in while the snow swirled in my headlights. Driving slowly, and extra cautiously, I made it to Interstate 89. Then the shitbox of a car decided it had had enough of me, the cold weather, or both. One minute the Datsun B-210 was moving at a steady fifty miles per hour, and the next it was coasting without power. Even the headlights were going dim. I steered the dying vehicle into the breakdown lane, turned off the headlights, and let the engine rest for a couple moments. When I turned the key to start it back up, all I heard was a sickening click. I tried activating the flashing hazard lights, but they too were dead. I later learned it was all because of a faulty alternator.

First the ditch, and now stranded on a snowy highway in the black of night. All this on Christmas Eve. Just two hours earlier, I had been as happy as I'd ever been, and now I was cold and miserable on the side of a highway that was almost devoid of cars.

I stood outside the car and stuck my thumb out whenever I saw headlights. And those headlights passed me by. I thought my days of hitchhiking were over after my many expeditions with Opie, and here I was—a proud landowner—reduced to begging for a ride.

Someone did eventually stop and give me a ride to White River Junction. Back on the highway, my next ride covered a good chunk of distance, taking me down to Putney, Vermont. By now it must have been 9:00 p.m., and I knew my parents would be worried, so I had the driver drop me at a gas station with a pay phone, and I called home. I didn't want my father to even think about driving up to Vermont in the snow, so I made the call short and just said I'd be late and they should not wait up. They wanted to ask questions, but I said I had to run and hung up.

I only had another couple hours to go, and I was sure some Good Samaritan would pick me up. And right off the bat, one did. The problem was he was in a truck, and next to him were two other passengers wedged in tight. He said I looked desperate, but all he could offer me was a ride in the open-air cargo bed. I accepted. There weren't exactly a lot of vehicles on the road on a snowy Christmas Eve. The truck driver asked where I was going, and when I said to a town next to Springfield, he said he'd be happy to take me directly to the house.

Those were the two coldest hours of my life, curled up in the fetal position on a steel sheet, blanketed by falling snow and probed by a piercing wind.

———

At my parents' house I staggered in with ice-encrusted eyebrows, numb toes, and a nose redder than Rudolph's.

My father had seen the truck's headlights pull into the driveway and then leave after dropping me off, so the first question he asked was "Where's your car?"

"In Vermont, not far from the cabin I bought."

Epilogue

Keep close to Nature's heart . . . and break clear away, once in a while, and climb a mountain or spend a week in the woods. Wash your spirit clean.

—John Muir

We are slow to realize water—the beauty and the magic of it.
—Henry David Thoreau

A couple years after I bought the cabin, my dad made a visit and he loved it. I was so happy for him, just watching how he strolled around the six acres, read one of his history books on the porch, and stared into the flames of our campfire at night. He had long since given up fishing, but I still wanted to show him one of my favorite little brook trout streams. I can see him standing next to me, shoulder to shoulder, peering down at the dancing current flowing by. There was no water between us anymore. I had matured, and he had probably changed a bit too. He was still the happy man he had always been, still loved people from all walks of life, still lit up a party when he could attend, but he was a bit more mellow. We no longer had those heated arguments from my early teenage years, although we still had our disagreements. But to his credit, he never put pressure on me regarding any big decisions, instead letting me be my own person and blaze my own trail. And if I screwed up, I knew he'd be in my corner. What more can you ask for in a friend, in a father?

He never stayed at the cabin again, but he often said to me, "Isn't it good to know the cabin and land are there? Even if you can't be there, just thinking about it is pleasure enough."

When I'm at the cabin pond, I often think of my Dad, because water was the setting of some of our best times together, even back in the days when I didn't think he liked me. From Lake Morey to the Meadows to Moosehead Lake, my dad indulged my passion for water, and he probably enjoyed it almost as much as I.

My mother and father took care of Lynn together until my mother's death in 2002. Then my father continued on his own, caring for Lynn with help from a wonderful aide named Wendy until he had heart surgery at age eighty. My brothers and I had the painful task of finding a nursing home for Lynn, knowing my dad could no longer lift her. When my father recovered from his surgery, he visited Lynn every day in the nursing home, caring for her himself from 2:00 p.m. through her dinner period to 7:00 p.m.

My father passed away in 2015 at age eighty-eight, and Lynn died not long after that, in 2016, forty years after her accident. Because of my parents and gifted caretakers, friends, and relatives, she received the best care possible.

I realize now that when a person is young and growing up, you are constantly observing—perhaps subconsciously—your parents or, for that matter, any older person you are close to. You see their flaws and their strengths. I was learning—cataloging really—the traits and habits of my father that I admired, slowly incorporating them into my day-to-day life. And isn't that what people mean when they say that another person lives on in their heart? You might catch yourself and think, *I just sounded exactly like my dad or mom,* or *I just reacted the same way they did.* If you're lucky and had a good role model, your journey is easier, your decisions sounder, and your courage overcomes your fears.

My dad demonstrated that there are talkers and there are doers, and he showed me attitude is everything. He really meant it when he said taking care of Lynn was a pleasure, and he really did celebrate the smallest of pleasures, like when he walked into my garden, salt shaker in hand, and took a bite out of a juicy tomato. And he could transport himself to places simply through the power of his mind; I'm certain he "visited" the cabin when I'd call him up and tell him about the latest endeavor, folly, or misadventure. And I think he did the same with Mark when they discussed his latest artwork or rare coin find, and with Bob when they talked of his latest birding discovery.

———

I've had this theory that some people manufacture problems to fill a void in their lives, maybe because they have too much time on their hands. That was never an issue with my dad. He once showed me what he did with small problems: He made the gesture of flicking a piece of lint off his shoulder, signifying that it meant so little in the grand scheme of things. He was a master at ignoring discomfort and grabbing fun wherever he could. A friend of my father's once told me, "Your dad exudes positivity, and does it in his own style, and with grace." He certainly had his own style. I would have given anything to see him when, at age eighty-four, he walked into his favorite bar and restaurant on Halloween night dressed in his minuteman garb, and whether it was true that the manager told him he had best put the musket back in his car.

When I want to take a shortcut on a project, I almost always hear my dad's voice saying, "Do it right," or "Are you sure about that?" When I bitch and moan about a problem, I catch myself, then try to solve it instead of making an art form of self-pity. When I'm wasteful, I think of how hard my dad worked at the bakery, and I become efficient and economical. When I'm lonely, I turn to my library, just like he did, and

I'm transported to another time and place. When I'm dealt a really raw deal and think I have no control, I stop myself and hear my dad say, "Wait a minute, you do have some control; you can control your *reaction*." I know my dad would have found a way to improve the bad situation, and I should do the same.

While I was writing this book, I had some family photographs I'd refer to from the time period. And in an envelope of photos, a scrap of paper fell out with my father's writing on it. It said, "By endurance, we conquer." That was him to a T.

Dad's determination could bend the bounds of normal human limitations.

———

The first couple of years at the cabin were filled with moments of joy, moments of terror, and a young man's overconfidence leading to one jam after another. I wrote about those early years in my book *There's a Porcupine in My Outhouse*, and many of those moments occurred with my brothers and old friends from Longmeadow. But when the book was finished, I felt I had left something out: What drove me to buy a cabin at age twenty-three, when friends were thinking of new cars and trips to distant lands? And in that earlier book, I never did acknowledge that there would be no cabin without my parents' encouragement and their loan (which I paid off in ten years rather than the five we originally agreed to).

Many of the first weekends at the cabin were spent working with an ax—cutting down smaller trees so that a little sunlight reached the A-frame and glimpses of the lake could be seen. The next year I was back at it, this time with a saw. I'd barely made a dent for the view I visualized, so the third year I bought a chainsaw. It was treacherous work, cutting hundred-foot-tall hemlocks and spruce crowded together on a slope, but I loved every minute of it. It took about twenty years, but eventually I carved out a view of the rolling mountain range to the west and some of the blue water below in the lake. New trees have taken the place of old ones, and some are now forty feet high.

I brought many friends, even a couple girlfriends, to the cabin during my twenties. Some loved the solitude; others were uncomfortable. Many were hesitant to swim in the pond (fears of the Loch Ness Monster?), even though it's one of the most pristine bodies of water on earth. Some guests looked over their shoulder for black bears when hiking, and almost all became a little freaked out by the silence of the night, occasionally pierced by an animal screaming or shuffling through the woods.

Later, I brought my two children to the cabin several times each summer. Consequently, both became comfortable in the wilderness and knowledgeable anglers. Their cabin indoctrination started as early as nine months old, when I'd have one of the kids in a baby backpack as I walked the edge of the pond fishing; I'd point out the different trees and plants, naming them. My daughter, Kristin, now works in finance in Hong Kong and London, and our annual trip to the cabin is the total change of pace she craves, saying, "It's like going to a different planet." And my son, Brian, a professional poker player who travels the world, loves nothing better than a swim in the pond and a beer on the deck.

For a type-A person like myself, who has been hyperactive from the get-go and has trouble sitting still, I find the cabin is the one place I shift into a lower gear I previously didn't know I had. I can sit for two hours on the deck in the late afternoon, watch cloud formations sail by the distant hills, and then take in the colors from the setting sun. If I move at all, it's to relight a cigar, grab a cold beer, or jot down a thought in the guest book. Then, when I can no longer see the hills opposite the pond, I'll have dinner, put a mattress on the screened porch, and read for a while. The barred owls start calling, the loon makes its mournful cry, and a coyote yips somewhere down the driveway. I might go back on the deck to see the stars, brighter than blazes with no light pollution, or I might fall asleep exhausted from a day tramping around or fishing in the fresh air.

The question I'm asked the most about the cabin is what changes I've made to it over forty years. The answer: not many. Original furniture that was in the cabin when I first snowshoed up with the Realtor is still there, including the ratty old couch and those incredibly comfy oak chairs with the big armrests. Opie helped me install insulation and then nail paneling over it on the walls. Then we had the bright idea of nailing—not hanging—large pieces of acoustic suspended ceiling tiles into the framework above us. Consequently, it bowed and buckled, and I observed to Opie that when we lay down to sleep, we could look up and pretend we were gazing at the ocean's waves. But another guest had a different take, "It looks like this was done by two guys who had too much to drink and were in a hurry to go fishing."

Nothing else was done to the inside. Friends suggested I make a loft out of the second floor, but I always found some excuse to avoid any more work inside the cabin, preferring to be outside. I did paint the exterior, and I had a carpenter expand the little porch into a screen porch and add a deck extending out over the cliff facing the pond. That was the smartest investment I made. Once that was done, I usually slept and ate on the porch or deck in the warm weather months and used the cabin itself for storage.

Although not a construction improvement, one rule I instituted from day one was that each guest should make an entry in the guest book. Early entries were short, about a paragraph or two, but after a couple years, people, myself included, were chronicling their entire stay in detailed multipage entries. Nine guest books have been filled over the years, and I love nothing better than to sit on the deck and laugh as I read visitors' tales of fun and tales of woe. Some of the writing is incredibly creative, and I think the guest book is an outlet for the writer in all of us. And those entries are useful as well. I hope to do a book about the later years at the cabin, and friends' comments will help jog my memory of the misadventures and mistakes we flatlanders made in the woods.

The million-dollar question of "What about plumbing?" usually gets a response from me of "What about it? Man lived for thousands of years without it." The truth is, the outhouse never bothered me, and I wanted to keep the cabin simple and not worry about a well, draining pipes at the end of autumn, and bringing in heavy machinery to dig a septic system. The cabin's simplicity makes it worry-free, and at the end of the "season," around mid-October, I simply shut the door.

I'm sixty-five now, and I still own the cabin. From a financial point of view, it was a terrible investment: a cabin mostly unoccupied, no rental income, high yearly taxes, and low price appreciation compared to other areas of the country. Had I put that money in the stock market, I would have made many times the appreciation of the cabin. And if I factor in real estate taxes paid, I broke about even on my cabin.

But the cabin has given me something the stock market never could have: adventures and pure joy. If you divide eighty-five hundred dollars by forty years of wonderful adventures, my purchase was a good one. Not all investments have to earn a monetary rate of return; some are paid in memories.

Acknowledgments

A GREAT MANY PEOPLE HELPED ME IN WRITING THIS BOOK, ESPECIALLY reconstructing events from days gone by. In fact, most everyone mentioned in the book helped me in one way or another, and they all have my gratitude for sharing memories and answering my many questions. My brother Mark and Alison O'Leary were especially generous with their time, proofreading and offering advice. And I'd like to thank my editor Eugene Brissie, copy editor Paulette Baker, production editor Kristen Mellitt, and publicist Ryan Meyer. The team at Lyons Press are true pros. Thank you.

Author's Note

The Waters Between Us was a multiyear project for me. The term "labor of love" is an apt one for this book, and writing it was a way to honor my parents, Lynn, and others who have passed away. I tried to be brutally honest in recalling special moments and events, even when it made me look selfish and shallow. I like to think I learned from those experiences and grew to be a better man.

In some cases, names have been changed to protect the guilty. Dialogue has been re-created to the best of my memory and ability. I was aided, however, by my lifelong habit of writing journals and diaries. Occasionally, I even wrote complete essays on particular events. Fortunately, I'm a pack rat and kept almost every piece of writing I've ever done, so before I sat down to tackle this book, I first organized all that material by year. It was a huge help in putting me back in the moment and into the setting of those natural places that mean so much to me.

For those parents reading this book who have a son or daughter that is on the wild side and causing your hair to go gray, don't give up. Hang in there like my father did. Some of us are late bloomers, and maturity is in a constant struggle with impulsiveness. Encourage independence, unsupervised activities, and time spent in the natural world away from adult pressures that will come soon enough.

My hope is that someday, long after I'm gone, a teenager will read *The Waters Between Us* and think, *So, I'm not the only one who gets a thrill from exploring the woods or discovering the secrets of a swamp.* Those hours outdoors are never wasted; they can soothe frazzled nerves and allow you to focus on what's important. Make your own adventures, and learn by trial and error. But remember, don't throw a rock at a moose or brag about your plan to canoe around a lake.

About the Author

Michael J. Tougias *(pronounced TOH-gis)* is a lecturer and *New York Times* best-selling author or co-author of thirty-one books for adults and six for young adults and children.

Fatal Forecast: An Incredible True Tale of Disaster and Survival at Sea was praised by the *Los Angeles Times* as "a breathtaking book—Tougias spins a marvelous and terrifying story." *The Finest Hours*, which Tougias co-authored, tells the true story of the Coast Guard's most daring rescue. A finalist for the Massachusetts Book Award, the book was made into a movie by Disney. *Ten Hours Until Dawn: The True Story of Heroism and Tragedy Aboard the* Can Do, was selected by the American Library Association as one of the "Top Books of the Year" and described as a "white-knuckle read, the best book of its kind." His latest books are *A Storm Too Soon, Rescue of the* Bounty *in Superstorm Sandy*, and *Above & Beyond*.

Several of Tougias's books have been adapted for middle readers (ages eight–thirteen) and for chapter books with MacMillan Publishers/ Christy Ottaviano Books, including *Into the Blizzard, Attacked at Sea, A Storm Too Soon*, and *The Finest Hours*.

Tougias has been featured on ABC's *20/20*, The Travel Channel, and the Weather Channel, among other TV appearances. He offers slide lectures for each of his books and speaks at libraries, lecture series, schools, and colleges across the country. He also speaks to business groups and associations on leadership and decision making, including such programs as Leadership Lessons from the Finest Hours, Survival Lessons: Decision Making Under Pressure, and Fourteen Steps to Strategic Decision Making: JFK and the Cuban Missile Crisis.

Tougias is currently at work on a sequel to *The Waters Between Us* and *There's A Porcupine in My Outhouse*. He lives in Florida and Massachusetts when not at his cabin in Vermont. For more information, videos of some of the rescues Tougias writes about, or to contact the author about speaking, visit michaeltougias.com.